NORTH of RELIANCE

A Personal Story of Living Beyond the Wilderness

NORTH *of* RELIANCE

A Personal Story of Living Beyond the Wilderness

Dave Olesen

NORTHWORD
PRESS, INC
MINOCQUA, WI 54548

For my father and mother,
James and Linnea Olesen

Allegiances

It is time for all the heroes to go home
if they have any, time for all of us common ones
to locate ourselves by the real things
we live by.

Far to the north, or indeed in any direction,
strange mountains and creatures have always lurked —
elves, goblins, trolls and spiders:—we
encounter them in dread and wonder,

But once we have tasted far streams, touched the gold,
found some limit beyond the waterfall,
a season changes, and we come back, changed
but safe, quiet, grateful.

Suppose an insane wind holds all the hills
while strange beliefs whine at the traveler's ears,
we ordinary beings can cling to the earth and love
where we are, sturdy for common things.

— William Stafford

Other books by Dave Olesen:
A Wonderful Country: The Quetico-Superior Stories of Bill Magie
Cold Nights, Fast Trails: Reflections of a Modern Dog Musher

The author is grateful for permission to quote "Allegiances" by William Stafford.

NorthWord Press, Inc.
P.O. Box 1360
Minocqua, WI 54548

Jacket design by Wayne Parmley
Layout and illustrations by Amy J. Monday
Cover photograph by Stephen J. Krasemann

Library of Congress Cataloging-in-Publication Data

Olesen, David.
     North of Reliance: a personal story of living beyond the wilderness / by David Olesen; photography by Kristen Olesen.
          p. cm.
          ISBN 1-55971-433-6
          I. Olesen, David. 2. Mushers--Northwest Territories--Biography.
3. Bush pilots--Northwest Territories--Biography. I. Title. SF440. 15.044 1994
971. 9303'092--dc20
[B]   94-12981
                                                                 CIP

Printed in U.S.A.
For a free catalog describing NorthWord's line of nature books and gifts, call 1-800-336-5666

TABLE OF CONTENTS

PREFACE

62 degrees, 51 minutes North; 109 degrees, 15 minutes West.

Imagine a map of the world. Draw a line straight north from Gallup, New Mexico, through Cody, Wyoming, and Red Lodge, Montana, past Swift Current, Saskatchewan, and on up from Lake Athabasca to the Arctic Ocean. Now find Mount McKinley in Alaska, and with an east-west line connect it to the southern tip of Baffin Island, or over the North Atlantic to Reykjavik and Lillehammer. Where those two lines cross, in the Northwest Territories of Canada, a small river called the Hoarfrost spills down from

the tundra into the northeast tip of a cold, vast lake.

The intersection, this place, is twelve miles north of a dot some maps and globes still show, a dot that is labeled "Reliance." That dot marks the site of an abandoned weather station and trading post. Reliance is both a physical point of reference and a suitable metaphor; my wife Kristen and I live twelve miles north of Reliance.

Sometimes I take my bearings by considering those two long lines. I face south and envision bands of antelope coursing the high plains of Montana, and I can almost see the peaks of the Beartooth Range. To my right, a thousand miles beyond the ridge there, I conjure up the mountains of Alaska and the wind-hammered villages along the Bering Sea. On my left, through the woods that slope back from the cabin, I try to imagine the cold ocean and the farms of Scandinavia where my great-grandfathers lived. Over my shoulder, straight north, more immediate and familiar than those other distant lands, stretch the barrens and pack ice, 1,870 miles to the Pole....

My expansive daydream dissolves; I am back at my desk. Out the window I see the small birches we transplanted last spring. Dry wood crackles in the stove at my side; its warmth soaks through my wool trousers.

This is home. It is easy enough to locate on paper, or in one's imagination, but on the inconvenient sprawling earth it is difficult to reach. Drive north a thousand miles from Edmonton to Yellowknife. From there hug the north shore of Great Slave Lake, fifth largest on the continent and the deepest body of fresh water in the Western Hemisphere. Carry on along that rocky coast for a week by boat or dogteam, or charter a bushplane and fly. Our homestead is 208 miles out, and in winter this is the first warm place you'll find in all those miles. On a broad sand beach under the brow of a steep bluff, facing stark cliffs across a wide bay, stand a couple of log cabins, a fenced-off garden, a timber and stone pier, some overturned boats and canoes, a barn and three dozen huskies, a meat cache on high stilts, two storage sheds, a sauna, and a pair of human beings.

In 1987, when I was thirty years old, I moved to the silence and severity of this place. I was looking for a new standpoint, a life more difficult and more direct. Amidst this dramatic beauty and pristine integrity, this opposition of power and fragility, I have not found precisely what I came seeking, but neither am I now the same person who first moved north to search. The place has changed me, as I suspected it would, and is changing me still.

This is the ragged northern edge of the continent; here is what remains of the frontier. A friend of mine begins his letters to me with "Greetings, Mars Colony." There is inspiration here, and there are daunting struggles, solitude, and occasional bewilderment. I have found a mate, Kristen, with whom to share it all. Together we get by.

On this last morning in November a fine-grained snow drifts down and the day's dim light silhouettes the spruces in a dull monochrome. I stand and type at my high shelf desk by the window. I have a few stories to tell, some thoughts to consider and events to describe. I am an immigrant, with a dispatch to send from a distant outpost.

David Olesen
Hoarfrost River, Canada
November 30, 1993

SOLSTICES

Two days in each year mean as much to me as any holiday, any birthday, any political or historical remembrance—in fact, mean more than most of those other dates ever do. These are the solstices, the "sun's standings." Each is a precise instant, almost nonexistent, like the two moments in the swing of a pendulum when the weight pauses at the ends of its arc.

The moment itself, the standing, is not what counts. I don't care precisely when spring becomes summer, or autumn becomes winter. It is not the standing still of the sun's arc in the sky that is significant, but the change in the trend of the days, and the shift of the year.

June 21.

The summer sostice, the start of summer in the northern hemisphere, is always for me the less festive of the sun's two standings. Bathed in endless light, with new leaves sparkling on the birches, the lakes melting and rapidly rising, geese and loons and ducks passing north, a batch of tiny, fast mosquitoes on the wing, the earth drinks up hour after hour, day after day of cool bright

1

sunlight. June twenty-first, or the twenty-second in some years, is marked on the calendar: "Summer Solstice" or "Summer Begins." A natural holiday! But a voice within me holds out and counsels reserve. This is the day of the change, it reminds me. The pendulum hangs at the top of its swing in the bright blaze of sunlight, and now, soon, the very next minute, it swings down and away, gathering speed, dropping toward darkness and cold.

On summer solstice for the past two years we have visited friends who manage the sport-fishing lodge in Reliance. It is not a planned ritual, but it is beginning to feel like one. We fly down to Reliance in our plane, on floats at that season, wind up staying for dinner and talking late into the evening. The sun dips lower and lower, its light first leaving the surface of the lake and then climbing the thousand-foot cliffs along the Kahochella Peninsula. By 11:30 P.M. or so, even the highest promontories to the west are all in shadow. The sun is down. One of us four notices it first, and we all lean to the broad porch windows as if to confirm and approve of it.

Bright daylight still pours over the rim of the horizon; there is no "legal darkness" at all, which begins when the sun dips more than six degrees below the horizon. The sun will edge along out of sight for about four hours, and rise again.

We sit and talk for another hour. At one in the morning Kristen and I get up, say our good-byes, and walk down to the dock where the little yellow plane is tied. Its windshield is opaque with dew in the chilled air above the cold water of Great Slave Lake. Kristen climbs in, I get the ropes untied and step onto the float. To start the motor, I grasp one blade of the propeller in a gloved hand, switch on the magnetos and pull downward. The engine catches, fires and dies. I prime it again, brace myself and tug. The motor catches and keeps firing; the plane eases away from the dock. Before I climb in I look back at the lodge to wave, but our friends have already gone to bed.

I check the controls and wipe the steam from the inner surface of the windshield. The plane chugs down the bay away from the six or eight people within earshot, all of them asleep. There is no wind. We turn out toward the open lake and at full throttle the small engine ambitiously fills the fjord with sound. Water arcs out from the chines of the floats as we gain speed, the plane accelerates and climbs onto the step, and with a nudge of back pressure on the control stick the wings lift us up from the lake.

We climb slowly in a gradual turn to the north. The view of the lake and the hills under the bright clear sky is intoxicating. Fields of broken ice pans, mottled white and purple, still clutter the expanse of McLeod Bay. Time slows; every moment feels ceremonial to me now, hungry as I am for ceremony on this solstice night. In a few minutes we are circling above our homestead, easing downward again and admiring the patch of open water that has formed at the mouth of the Hoarfrost. A light breeze flows down the river valley, ruffling the water's surface, as it will on almost every calm night of the summer.

We swoop low over the edge of the disintegrating ice, slowing as we turn into the breeze. A reassuring patter marks our touchdown; the heels of the floats toss long plumes of spray to each side. The plane slows and settles down, the engine ticking softly as we taxi in. The floats grate softly on the sand beach. We tie down the plane and walk up to the cabin.

It is solstice. We must wait for sunrise. I put on the teapot and we read our mail, accumulated over the weeks of break-up when we could not reach Reliance.

At three o'clock in the morning I step outside. It is dawn. The sun is shining on the hills across the bay, lighting them at an angle which we are rarely awake to see, throwing the cliffs into new patterns of relief and shadow.

Summer solstice, the standing still, is past. We have all turned toward winter again. It is dawn and time to sleep, and there is a heaviness in the pit of my stomach. White-throated sparrows sing as the sunlight of summer's beginning grows steadily stronger.

The days will dwindle almost imperceptibly at first, and a brief period of darkness will come back by late July. We climb into the brightly lit loft and draw the shades around our bed. In a few hours the strong sunbeams wake us. Fuzzy after the short sleep, I will get up and put on the coffee; start the day, start the long slide down the back half of the year.

December 22.

Half-light. It is nine in the morning and I'm out in the dogyard scooping frozen dog droppings into a big metal pail. The droppings are like round stones; it is thirty-seven degrees below zero. The dogs are noisy and excited. I have just doled out their morning ration of fish broth and a few of them are still working the dents and corners of their battered pans, looking for a fleck of whitefish they might have missed. "Easy there, Blondie, it's cold out. You'll stick your tongue right to that bowl." My words are

3

futile, of course—a couple of seconds later I see that her pan is spotted with frozen drops of blood. Grayling, her grizzled old neighbor, looks at me with what could pass for a knowing smile.

It is still dark enough that I can clearly see the bright circle of light before the cabin window. The sky is a deep blue, almost indigo, and there is ice fog in the air, a thick haze formed by frozen water vapor. I am dressed heavily in bulky army-surplus flight pants, a thick sweater under a pullover parka, a suit of wool underwear beneath it all, a big fur hat, enormous insulated boots, and thin cotton chore gloves now stiff with frozen fish broth. This is miserable; although I'm warm otherwise, my fingers are numb. I set the bucket down, kick the blade of the shovel into the hard-packed snow, and walk to the cabin.

"It's like winter out there," I say to Kristen as I dig out a thick pair of mittens and leather choppers. I wrap my bare hands right around the pipe of the woodstove, flirting with the hot metal and heating my aching fingers. My face flushes and tingles in the warmth of the house. In a few minutes I turn back out to finish the chores.

It *is* winter as of this morning, the twenty-second of December. This is it; this is as dark as it's going to get. There is comfort in that thought.

Darkness has become a habit now. After the two woodstoves, the lights are the most vital fixtures in the cabin. A battery-powered headlamp seems to have permanently sprouted from each of our foreheads, to light our work outdoors. Lately we have been luxuriating in the use of small electric lights indoors as well, running the gasoline-powered electrical generator to keep the bank of batteries charged. Every evening we have been using a drill or circular saw or sewing machine, repairing sleds and making new harnesses for the dogs. Those tools require the generator and there is current to spare. When the projects are finished we will be more thrifty and revert to gas lamps filled with abandoned jet fuel from an old fuel cache nearby.

With the holidays of Christmas and New Year's just ahead, we will pass this solstice day without much change in our winter routine. There are the chores first, then breakfast, and today a careful recording of the time of sunrise. By some astronomical phenomenon which I've never quite grasped, this is the shortest day of the year, but this morning is not the year's latest sunrise. The dawn continues to come later by a minute or two until the first week in January, but the sunsets have already begun to shift. The gap between the two, the duration of the day, now begins to widen.

At 10:05 the first ray of direct sunlight is visible on the southeast

4

horizon, a brilliant sliver just edging the skyline above Pike's Portage. Creeping along the line of the hills, imperceptibly climbing, the sun slowly appears. Red through the icy haze, it looks this morning like the distant star that it is—millions of miles away, throwing a wan light toward the earth. Somehow, in the eight minutes or so since that light started toward us, it seems to have lost all vestiges of warmth. The sun is up, but the air seems even colder now.

At 1:30 in the afternoon, the little zipper-pull thermometer on the handlebar of my sled reads minus thirty-five. Our four hours and twenty minutes of sunlight are nearly gone—the mirror image of those four hours that we spent staring out the window, flying home, and reading our mail last June. Low in the south-southwest, twin sundogs flank the sun on either side, apparitions created by crystals of ice high in the atmosphere.

Ahead of me beneath the line of sundogs, eight sled dogs are in a burst of speed, heading for home, rounding the point southeast of the cabin. My cheeks and nose are suddenly stung by the thick cold air that flows down the river bottom, and I raise my beaver-fur mitt to my face. The team's enthusiasm has come too soon, and they cannot hold their gallop. They drop back into a trot and I can lower my mitten. The breath of the lead dogs flows like smoke back over the team and rimes the sled cover with frost. The sun slips closer to the horizon.

We start across the inlet at the rivermouth. About a mile to the west I see Kristen pass the opposite headland, her team turning for home. I smile; it will be a race. I pull out the jingler and rattle it with a growling "Get up!" My dogs reluctantly break into a lope again. I see Kristen pedaling behind her team, and I start pedaling too.

Then I remember, and we are taxiing in, the door of the plane open, water gurgling softly beneath the floats, crossing this same piece of lake by the homestead at 2:30 in the morning on June 22. For just a moment the sun stands still. My mukluk squeaks on the packed snow as I nudge the planet forward toward the welcome light of another year.

LIGHTING OUT

When I was a high-school student in Crystal Lake Illinois, 45 miles northwest of Chicago, I devoured books filled with passages like this from *The Big Sky* by A.B. Guthrie: "Jim rode down the valley of the Teton where the stream turned north. He climbed the far slope and halted his horse on the high nose that separated the Teton from the Missouri. He saw Fort McKenzie below him, with only three tepees pitched about. Beyond it the Missouri flowed wide, shining silver in the sun."

Bursting with restlessness, I harbored a relentless envy for those real and fictitious men of the old Northwest: Colter and Bridger, Deakins and Caudill, the mountain men and free traders who worked flatboats and canoes up the Missouri and the Yellowstone. A.B. Guthrie's novel, *The Big Sky*, is an archetype for me; I return to it over the years to savour its scenes again and again with a boyish, vicarious thrill.

In the final decades of the twentieth century I have done what I can to realize that old dream. If there is an archetypal Northwest remaining in the world, I am certainly living within one corner of it. Wildness and the North survive here, unfettered, brooding, and powerful.

I first encountered the far north in Illinois, among some abandoned gravel pits five miles from the town of Crystal Lake. The pits had been abandoned by the dredging companies, and over the years they had filled up with clear turquoise water that stayed clean and cold all summer. Bluegills and smallmouth bass flourished there, and my friends and I learned to fly-fish for them. Surrounding the deep ponds and connecting streams were stark sand ridges that could have been barrenland eskers, dotted with small clumps of trees and shallow swales where grass had taken root. Between the gravel pits and the road where we parked our bicycles lay two pastures, occupied on most early mornings by a cantankerous bull and a herd of cattle.

Crossing those pastures in the twilight before dawn cut us off completely from the comfortable suburbia of Crystal Lake. Once out beyond the pasture fences I could taste a vestige of the remoteness and hard-bitten simplicity that I have always admired in landscape. There was the magical mix of clear cold water, untracked sand and stone, sparse vegetation, and sky. Those scooped-up, picked-over terminal moraines of the last Ice Age still gave forth some of the clarity and freshness of the distant North, as if the giant shovel blades had uncovered a slumbering glacial spirit and set it free to roam for a few years there.

Today the outskirts of Crystal Lake have been "developed," made over into sod-lawned housing developments: Turnberry, Lake-In-The-Hills, and Coventry Green. "Where they cut down all the trees and name streets after them," as my father summarized it. In the mid-1970s the town of Crystal Lake began to engulf and obliterate the gravel pits and farms that once surrounded it. The people there shop in new malls and commute to work on the expressways. The cattle we used to dodge were shipped long ago to a meat packer.

Those places that first showed me what I wanted and loved are gone, but I am lucky. I got an early taste of the North, and after that I only had to trust my compass.

My track was not direct from the pastures and moraines of Illinois to the cliffs around McLeod Bay. I came north and west in stages, by way of a two-year stay in Montana and a ten-year stopover in Minnesota and Wisconsin. Even in those waypoints my bent was obvious—the border lakes of Minnesota and the high country of Montana are provinces of the North. Duluth and Missoula are border towns. Upward from them, whether in altitude or latitude, one enters another country: spruce trees, trout lakes, mosquitoes, forty-below nights, bare granite, sled dogs. The northern fringe of the Midwest States straddles the great Canadian Shield. In fact, more than half of all *Canadians* live in cities farther south than Ashland, Wisconsin.

In the summer of 1980 I was twenty-two years old. With my friend and mentor Duncan Storlie, I arrived on a little lake outside of Ely, Minnesota. We pitched a tipi on a high bare ridge and began to build a log cabin on a forty-acre parcel of second-growth poplar. On a spur of smooth bedrock out in front of the tipi we passed long summer evenings around a small fire. Our muscles ached from the day's lessons with chainsaw, drawknife, and green logs. We laughed often, and that summer I fell in love for the first time—with a woman, briefly, and with a way of life forever. As freeze-up came on and the snow fell, I moved from the tipi indoors to the snug cabin we had built. Duncan left for the Twin Cities, and with a handful of sled dogs for companions I began to live full-time in the northwoods.

For the next three years Stump Lake was my home. I see now that those years were my apprenticeship. I learned to net fish and hunt animals, learned about sled dogs and woodstoves and root cellars. I learned too about isolation, solitude, and loneliness. The cabin was only a mile or so from the nearest road, and on summer evenings I could hear traffic in the distance, but being at the far end of a rough, indistinct trail introduced me to a frame of mind that has since become all too familiar. I passed my days alone at Stump in a mood of constant anticipation, craving visitors and conversation as fiercely as I craved solitude and silence.

From Stump Lake I could envision a life farther north. I could make a leap of imagination and trust that it was at least partly accurate. On annual trips to the sub-Arctic I fleshed out my visions of the far north, always returning to the little cabin and to the various jobs I held during those years—guiding, woodcutting, and pumping fuel at the local airport. Year by year my starry-eyed infatuation with log-cabin life was tempered by its realities, yet I remained in love with it as the lessons built upon each other.

I could have stayed at Stump Lake for years, but the land and the cabin were not truly my own, and I began to want ownership. There was land for sale north and west of Ely, up the Echo Trail toward the Ontario border. Sections long owned by the U.S. Steel Corporation had at last been deemed expendable by the corporate land agents. A few of the tracts had burned in a recent forest fire, and the prices on those were low. Those prices matched my means, and as I walked among the bare granite and charred stumps, the open expanses and sheer contrariness of the place sparked my imagination. In partnership with others I submitted a bid, but someone else offered more than we did. I could have lived there happily, I think, in a cabin on the burned-over hillside, watched as the new growth reclaimed the slopes year by year, and enjoyed the irascibility and freshness of my choice.

That was as close as I ever came to staying in northern Minnesota. I looked at many other remote acreages, walked them on snowshoes, and flew over them in an airplane. I lived in cabins and tents on land owned by friends, and in a run-down trailer at the school where I taught winter camping courses. In 1982, I subscribed to the weekly Yellowknife newspaper, and in November of that year I read a small advertisement for a titled lot on the East Arm of Great Slave Lake. The location was left vague, but the address for inquiries was "Hoarfrost Holdings, Ltd." I remembered the Hoarfrost River; I had studied its watershed on the map when I passed through Reliance by dogteam in the spring of 1981. I was interested.

Northern Canada has always appealed to me more than the State of Alaska. In a pattern that has kept my life both interesting and unorthodox, I have always tended to reject the common thinking. If one lives in the United States, and one wants to move to the far north, one moves to Alaska—that is the standard progression. There are no immigration applications to be made, and all that is required is a good dose of gumption and a vehicle capable of making it to Anchorage or Fairbanks. That move seemed straightforward and relatively simple to me; it was the logical move for a person with my background and my cravings. It was clearly the sensible thing to do, and therefore I had no desire to do it.

Instead I made plans to visit the land that was for sale at the mouth of the Hoarfrost River. In July 1983, I voyaged out from Yellowknife to have a look at it, with a friend and ten dogs in an old wooden boat. We turned south again in September, and I thought then that I was finished with the Hoarfrost River scheme. The "700 square foot" cabin there had turned out to be a motley haphazard shack, and the asking price for the one-acre parcel of sand surrounding it was far beyond my reach. I tried to put it out of my mind, and I began again to search for a more accessible alternative near my family, my friends, and the work I had.

But northern Minnesota was changing. It was in the throes of becoming conscious of its own desirability—always a harbinger of strange deeds.

Long a haven for a footloose class of young, energetic people who came to work in summer camps or with the Forest Service, the Boundary Waters country emerged from the wilderness-protection battles of the late 1970s with a stamp of approval from urban refugees (myself among them, lest I forget).

I began to hear a clannish, affected "we" in the intonations of my peers: "We're proud of our heritage of wilderness and simple lifestyles," "here in our pristine groves of old-growth pine." I was suspicious. In a confusion that I have not yet resolved, I greeted with warmth and respect the loggers, miners, and pilots I knew, and met with cynical skepticism the canoe-topped Subarus and Toyotas rolling in from the Twin Cities.

By 1985 in Ely I could duck in to a new restaurant built of varnished logs, "The Chocolate Moose," for a lunch of bean sprouts and tunafish, or I could stop by on an August night for the Mesquite Chicken Barbeque. If I wanted to paddle into "The Boundary Waters Canoe Area Wilderness Area" [sic] on a canoe trip, I needed to apply in advance for a permit. The Dayton's Department Stores in Minneapolis introduced their *Boundary Waters* clothing collection, every outfit emblazoned with the embroidered image of a loon.

I was twenty-seven. I owned a rusty three-quarter-ton truck, a 1946 Piper Cub, an airplane hangar filled with what looked like the aftermath of an explosion, and twenty sled dogs staked out behind a rented one-room cabin. I was making a good living then, flying in the summer and running sled dogs in winter, building cabins and cutting wood and planting trees in the spring and fall. It was a glorious life, and as I looked ahead I could see clearly how it would all unfold. I found such clarity terrifying; something had to be done.

For a few weeks I seriously explored the prospect of signing on with the U.S. Navy as an officer-pilot candidate. Fortunately, I had a fleeting moment of insight clear enough to convince me that joining the Navy meant more than a chance to fly jets and see the world. I saw myself boarding a monstrous military-corporate battleship with Ronald Reagan at the helm, a ship hellbent on the destruction of everything I cherished. I stopped returning the recruiter's calls. Three weeks later I flew to Yellowknife, and with my savings bolstered by a loan and a profitable exchange rate on Canadian currency, I bought the little one-acre parcel of land I'd looked at in 1983, the place at the mouth of the Hoarfrost River.

With title and survey in my pocket I returned to Ely and slowly prepared to move north. After two years of applications, interviews, and clearances I was granted permission to take up permanent residence in Canada. The diplomat who finally gave me my papers was bemused by my destination. With a twinkle in his eye he suggested that instead of the required medical exam, he would in my case require a psychiatric assessment. Chuckling, he signed the forms.

Like Huck and Tom, I could light out for the Territories.

Having served my apprenticeship in the northwoods of Minnesota, in July of 1987 I arrived again by boat at the mouth of the Hoarfrost River. My father was with me; in quiet amazement he set about carrying piles of broken glass, cardboard boxes, dirty diapers, and spent 30/30 cartridges from the interior of my dream home. The cabin had been used only in passing, by a few hunters and trappers. Some eastbound canoeists stayed for a few days with us and helped fashion some small windows to light the dark room. We cut trees and built a crude boat ramp, chinked walls with mortar, staked out my dogs, and strung a radio antenna. Everything we did felt immediate and necessary; there weren't enough hours in the day. We worked from dawn to dusk, which in early August here yields an eighteen-hour day.

After two weeks my father left—he was a high-school teacher and classes were soon to start. I awoke in a sleeping bag on the floor of the cabin the next morning, alone at the place I had held in my mind for so long. This was not Stump Lake. I could not hear any cars in the distance.

That initial flurry of frantic activity took years to wind down. It still returns at certain seasons, and we dash around the place repairing, refining, gathering, building, and provisioning. During those times there is little contemplation of motives. The demands and preparations and improvements fill entire days.

I had learned years ago, though, at the little cabin on Stump, that at least one popular notion of rustic log-cabin life is mistaken. As seasons pass one's days are less filled with mundane, repetitive tasks. The daily chores which dilettantes and visitors imagine to be so all-consuming—splitting wood, hauling water, feeding dogs—are nothing. I am certain that I spend no more time working to heat my home, for instance, than does anyone who lives in a bungalow in Yellowknife or Duluth. My work is direct, with saw and sled and axe; that other person's work is at a job, where hour by hour they earn the cash that buys their heat. It all works out at least even, and I enjoy the afternoons I spend up the hill north of the homestead, cutting and stacking wood alongside the trails, so that we can stop the dogs near the end of a training run and load the sled. I would not happily sell those hours in order to purchase my warmth.

My apprenticeship is done, but I am still a journeyman here. Mastery lies somewhere ahead, or so I hope. Mastery will be making a living here, and making a good life of it. As Annie Dillard wrote in *The Writing Life*: "There is no shortage of good days. It is good lives that are hard to come by." I am unsure of the specific of the living that can be made here. There is a new course to be charted.

The life of the trapper, that one livelihood which has sustained men of my race in this country over the past hundred years, is for me a dead end. There are legal and political obstacles for me there, but even aside from those I have no desire to master those skills. I will kill a furry animal once every few years to make from its pelt a warm hat or a pair of mitts. One spring we trapped seven marten from our back pantry, in a flurry of revenge after a winter of depredations. That might be more than five hundred dollars worth of fur. On some days it is tempting to take up with it, to set lines and make my rounds. But I don't. There are other ways to earn a living here, along paths I have already begun to learn—piloting, guiding, writing, and mushing dogs. Time will tell.

I generate more questions than answers. I came here with no burning desire to escape, to shut myself away and turn my back on civilization. Such notions creep into my thoughts more frequently now, seven years into this, than they ever did at the outset. At times I see there is no choice. Even in the age of two-way radio and Twin Otters, sheer distance and contrast and day-to-day concerns cut us off completely from the society we left. But when I feel myself leaning too far toward the outlook of the hermit, toward notions of "just me and the missus and my AK-47," as Bill McKibben once described the credo of survivalists, I draw back in suspicion. That is the deadest of dead ends.

Yet we do our share of old-fashioned, outmoded pioneering as we attempt to make a home in this wilderness. With axe and chainsaw and shovel, wheelbarrow and dynamite, gillnet and rifle, we have established our place here. We have changed the character of this beach and these woods, cut new trails through the hills, fed and housed and clothed ourselves. We cut, kill, burn, and harvest our way through the years, just like the rest of humanity.

Life here now is a parade of paradoxy. Timeless arctic tools and scenes are daily juxtaposed with the latest gadgets: a team of huskies pulls up alongside a sleek snowmobile; the shimmering diaphanous veil of the aurora borealis is bisected by the strobelights of a 747. Sand and styrofoam, birch and polyethylene.

Reliance. I have always liked the ring of that word. When I stop and think about it, though, my fondness for it makes no sense. What the word connotes for me is not its meaning but its antonym. I insert a "self-" ahead of it so deftly that the prefix becomes a part of the meaning. But I do not live near "Self-Reliance."

What did Captain George Back mean when in 1833 he named his base camp at the head of Charlton Bay "Fort Reliance"? Reliance on what, Captain, or upon whom? Other old posts had names that rang with more bravado and optimism: Fort Enterprise, Fort Resolution, Fort Good Hope, to name three in the Northwest Territories. But Reliance?

From his *Narrative of the Arctic Land Expedition,* I find some insight: "On the 5th of November we had the pleasure of changing our cold tents for the comparative comfort of the house, which, like most of those in this country, was constructed of a framework, filled up with logs let into grooves, and closely plastered with a cement composed of common clay and sand... As every post in the country is distinguished by a name, I gave to ours that of Fort Reliance, in token of our trust in that merciful Providence, whose protection we humbly hoped would be extended to us in the many difficulties and dangers to which these services are exposed."

Back was not fooling himself. He was no arctic tenderfoot, and on his earlier expedition he had endured a few of the highlights of British barrenland exploration: forced marches, frostbite, a crew of mutinous starving voyageurs on the brink of murder and cannibalism. He knew what he was up against, and he clearly knew upon whom he relied: "merciful Providence."

If I am to be as forthright as Back, I must confess our own reliance. We rely, when all is said and done, on that modern petroleum-fueled industrial civilization, whose protection we humbly hope will be extended to us in the many difficulties and dangers to which these services are exposed. When, in a cynical pass, I sweep aside all the poetry of life in the northern wilderness, it can emerge as only an aberration of the same life and the same dependencies that now characterize life in Everytown, North America. "We're just consumers, you know," my neighbor Lance reminded me one morning at his trapping cabin on the barrens.

With my chainsaw I buck firewood. I pour fuel into the airplane and fly to town, there to order groceries and mail letters. We fire up the generator and washing machine, pump water up to the barn with our new hoses. This year, propane lights. Next year, perhaps, a new outboard motor. And can I synthesize propane or gasoline, design and build a battery bank or a photovoltaic panel? Hell, I haven't even learned to overhaul a carburetor.

I grumble with doubt as to the real advantage of such "labor-saving" devices as our washing machine, our outboard motors, and the old chain-saws with which I fell trees and build cabins, but I grumble only in the silence that descends when they break down. When they roar to life, re-fueled and repaired, burning gas and puffing exhaust fumes into this clean dry air, I go to work.

I have not come to self-reliance. I did not move here in order to make my own soap or chip stone arrowheads. I rely. My reliance is only a step detached from the moment-to-moment reliance that characterizes life in a highrise apartment. We are slightly north of that obvious reliance, but we can see it from here if we take an honest look.

I proposed marriage to Kristen one morning with the thermometer at fifty-two below zero. We were sitting by the south window in the little eight-by-eight cabin we'd built that first autumn at the Hoarfrost, "the cracker box," our neighbors called it. It was February, the month that always looms as a troublesome one in the northern bush. More feuds, petty disputes, grand schemes, vicious gossip, and sweeping changes have been born in February than in all other months of the year combined. It is a month to endure, and a month to be careful.

We were trying to see the future that morning. Kristen had been invit-ed to join a group of six women who would paddle the 600 miles of the Back River the following summer. It was a choice, and it brought into focus the question that was looming over us that February: what to do when winter ended? When there was more to do each day than buck wood, stoke stoves, cut new trails and run the dogs, what would we do? Spring was coming. Already the daylight lasted until 5:30 in the evening, a two-hour gain from the solstice.

"We could get married." That is how I first broached the idea. Casually, as if I'd said, "We could build a shed," or "we could enter that race in Fort McMurray."

Kristen asked me to repeat myself. I gazed out through the double-paned window at the thermometer, still stuck at fifty-some below, and back at the lovely dark-haired woman with the skin peeling from a recent frostbite on the tip of her nose, that nose that had been split down the middle by the handlebar of a sled almost exactly a year earlier, on a steep drop to the Yanert River valley in Alaska.

"Will you marry me?"

Silence. A pinging from the sheet-metal stove.

"Yes."

February was beaten, and our days here took a giant step more deeply into permanence. Now year by year I watch the log walls of that tiny cabin weather and darken. I will always remember that there, right there, we decided to get married.

A few nights later I passed the news out over the high-frequency radios: "Kristen and I are going to get married." Richard Black's voice crackled back from his camp seventy miles to the east: "Well, now you'll have someone to keep you warm all your years at the Hoarfrost."

A Lighting Out will, one hopes, lead to an Arrival. The lighting is the easy part; the arrival takes years. A part of arriving here has been to get a clear view of my motives; another part is the comprehension of my range. What is the extent of my territory? Where will I concentrate my efforts?

If a person owns a certain acreage, that must be a help. This forty, this quarter-section, this yard and garden plot help to focus and narrow the attention. Here I own a single acre, a square 200 feet on a side. Beyond that in all directions lies uninhabited land and lake, all belonging to that vague Canadian government entity, The Crown. Of course my range must spill out beyond this acre. Learning how far it goes in any given direction is a part of finally arriving here.

It is taking me a long time to grasp the scale of this country. Its resources are more sparsely scattered than were those of my old stomping grounds. The animals that live here have a wider range; the fish grow slowly and do not make such dependable and prolific spawning runs. Soil is a precious rarity, and the trees grow tall only in sheltered pockets of fertile ground. Stands of stunted, twisted spruce cover most of the lowlands and dwindle to a few hardy individuals on the ridgetops.

The enormity and emptiness of the country at first inspired me with visions of a huge territory. I would learn it all, from Aylmer Lake to the Thelon River, south beyond the Snowdrift River, west to the roadheads at Resolution and Yellowknife. Flying my small plane helped bolster those early notions of a vast range, but the longer I live here the smaller my territory becomes. The part of the landscape that feels truly familiar to me, and those certain places that have gained a personal significance—here I killed a moose, here we camped in that storm—is much more limited than those first grandiose visions would have had it.

Country seen from an airplane, however low and intricate the flight, is not truly encountered. Only when I slow down and walk, stand behind a team of dogs, or paddle along in a canoe can I conform the input of impressions to my capacity for interpretation and memory. It is only that realm within which I need no map, in which if pressed I could draw a map, that will become my range. From anywhere within it I could always find my way home, on foot or by canoe, with no supplies en route.

In his essay "Walking" Henry David Thoreau wrote: "There is in fact a sort of harmony discoverable between the capabilities of the landscape within a circle of ten miles' radius, or the limits of an afternoon walk, and the threescore years and ten of human life. It will never become quite familiar to you."

I differ a bit with his limits—twenty miles, round trip, being more than an afternoon walk for me, but his idea is accurate. In every season since I arrived here I have found myself for one reason or another in some spot ten miles or less from our cabin, but as new and unfamiliar to me as the headwaters of the Nahanni or the coast of Labrador. I pull into beaches I have never seen before, or follow flocks of ptarmigan into a hidden stand of tall, straight spruce. Despite its paucity of species and the relatively simple chains and webs among them, despite its straightforward geology and steady, dependable climate, this land still overwhelms my ability to know any more than a tiny tract of it.

Thoreau's circle of 315 square miles, when skewed by the shape of the shoreline and the slant of these northeast-running watersheds, is the approximate size of my range. The area takes me well up the Hoarfrost beyond treeline, in a swath a few miles wide. It runs east and west along the coast of the big lake, and up other drainages I have come to know. Those creeks have no names on the map; we know places by the names we have given them: Hawk Owl Creek, The Big Burn, Windy Lake, Obelisk.

My restlessness has met its match. Gradually those old envies, that feeling that perhaps I was born too late, slips away. I lit out; at last I begin to settle. In *The Big Sky*, A.B. Guthrie summed it up well: "The feel of the country settled into Jim, the great emptiness and age of it, the feel of westward mountains old as time and plains wide as forever and the blue sky flung across. The country didn't give a damn about a man or any animal. It let the buffalo and the antelope feed on it and the gophers dig and the birds fly and men crawl around, but what did it care, being one with time itself? What did it care about a man or his hankerings or what happened to him? There would be other men after him and others after them all wondering and all wishful and after a while all dead...He clucked to his horse and rolled in the saddle to its downhill jolt."

LA FOULE

The ravens are the first sign. One of us will be outside early in the morning and see them overhead, or we will hear them from inside the house, squawking and hooting as a late October day begins. If there are more than half a dozen ravens flying above our place on an autumn morning, a walk up the hill is a worthwhile check. If, as happened last year, twenty-three of them pass overhead from west to east, then it is all but certain. The caribou have come.

The barren-ground caribou are the lifeblood of this land; like blood they flow and carry, pulse and pause, enrich and sustain. The land without them is austere and more truly barren, more a place of physics than biology, a meager, scrawny, rocky place.

For summer visitors new to the country, the caribou—though far away at that season—still account for the most prevalent signs of animal life. Their small black droppings persist and accumulate, seeming never to decompose. Their trails wind everywhere through the bush—in the hour-long passage of a small herd across a patch of fragile lichen a century of growth is trampled; the passage of those animals over that place in that one

19

hour will be there to read for decades. Antlers litter the countryside, bleached bows three feet long, dropped in November as the bulls just out of rut wend exhausted and lean through the taiga forest.

I will never forget the most dramatic migration I have seen. Our awareness of it came almost by accident. On a Sunday walk up one of our trails, out to relax and to exercise a litter of pups, we crossed a fresh track in an inch of new snow. The tracks of a caribou hoof are rounded, almost circular, and distinct from the parallel prints of a moose. Caribou belong to the deer family; most barren-ground caribou are about the size of mule deer, or small adult whitetails. This was the track of a caribou, but only one. We walked on. Suddenly from up ahead we heard the clatter of antlers.

At that season, late October, every mature male caribou that moves along with the herd is prepared for a duel at the slightest provocation. It is breeding season. One bull will begin to trail along behind a cow, lowering his head and grunting in undignified tones, sounding more like a frog or a pig than a caribou. If he passes another bull they both freeze, lower their heads nearly to the ground, and turn as if to look away. Then, like two hockey players at a face-off, their heads come up, antlers engage, there is a rattle, a grunt, a scuffle for better footing, another collision, and it is over. The cow has wandered off. The bulls move on and the herd closes ranks around them.

That clatter of antlers filled the woods ahead of us. Four or five such duels were constantly in progress. The woods were filled with caribou. The movement that day was from east to west. There must have been a wide phalanx of animals sweeping in from the northeast, deflected by the open water of McLeod Bay. The main herd, as we were to find out the second day, forded the Hoarfrost about two miles upstream from the lake. Some of the caribou, not to be deterred by a mere ten miles of frigid water, actually waded out past the shorefast ice and began swimming south. All but one that I saw enter the water turned back, but that one bull swam steadily south until I lost sight of his great antlers miles out from shore. For all I know he swam clear across the lake.

With the animals so close to the lake and the boat, we decided to shoot two caribou there, where the work of getting them home would be easiest. When hunting caribou for food a cardinal rule is to act immediately. A hunt put off for another day too often turns up nothing, since the herd may disappear as instantly and unexpectedly as it arrives.

I shot two yearlings, whose meat would not be tainted by the scent of rutting season. With the pups excitedly nosing around, we gutted the caribou and dragged them back to the boat. Arriving home at dusk, I was glad to have the meat, and glad to have put behind us that practical aspect of the great herd's dramatic appearance.

The next morning we set out from the cabin at first light, north up the hill. The half-lit woods were alive with grunts and snorts, the collision of antlers, and the breaking of branches. On the edge of an open bench a mile above our home, we hid ourselves within a thicket of spruce and watched. Group after group, in pairs, trios, and dozens—bulls, cows, and calves—emerged into the broad clearing, looked almost carelessly to each side, and filed past us at a distance of six to ten feet. Never before had I seen caribou at such close quarters. This, I thought, was how hunters had been able to spear these animals, and to take them easily with arrows. This was how, in times of need, they could even be snared.

The caribou passing us were rimed with ice. Some paused to shake themselves, like retrievers coming ashore to a duck blind. Kristen gestured to me, *they must be swimming the river*. We walked east toward the Hoarfrost, against the flow of the herd.

The view from a rock outcrop a hundred feet above the river was breathtaking. Never before or since have I stood on the ground and seen such a tide of animals. Lined up along the Hoarfrost, stretching east up into the hills, fording the river in an unbroken procession six and eight abreast, pairs of bulls skirmishing on the thin strips of ice along the river-bank, calves being swept downstream into a rapids, paddling frantically across the current amidst haystacks and rollers of ice-cold water, their heads bobbing and finally their shoulders emerging, climbing out on spindly legs and moving on... a steady stream of caribou. We stood silent-ly and stared for a long time. I felt the rapt attention that comes when a dream is being realized. This sight was a part of what I had moved north to find. *La Foule*, the voyageurs had called them—"the throng."

My trance was broken as Kristen began aiming and shooting with her camera. I tried an experiment. I shut my eyes, turned and shifted my head, and opened my eyes again. Wherever my gaze happened to rest there were caribou in sight. I got out my watch, sat down, and began counting.

In three minutes, eighty-three caribou crossed the Hoarfrost in one place, the main fording spot just below Lacy Pond. Upstream of them and down through two sets of rapids, I knew that other lines of animals were crossing. Just to be conservative I knocked the tally back to an average rate of fifty in three minutes, up and down the half-mile of river within our view. That was a thousand caribou per hour passing that place. This had been going on since the previous afternoon, and it showed no sign of slacking off. Twenty-four thousand in twenty-four hours? If I used my figure of eighty-three and went up from there to a hundred in three minutes, accounting for all the caribou that were passing other fording places up and down from where I had counted, my estimate came to 48,000 in twenty-four hours.

I wished that I could climb into my plane and fly above the herd to ascertain the true dimensions of this huge movement. But the Cub was parked on the beach in front of the cabin, its floats already stored for the season, its skis shimmed up on the sand and facing the waves of the open lake. There would be no aerial view.

Kristen and I each wandered alone for the next few hours. Immersed in the spectacle, moving through it from rock to outcrop to meadow to riverbank, taking photographs and just standing still for long minutes at a time, the day passed quickly. In late afternoon I met Kristen again, up on the rock overlooking the river. She had photographed the fording place and had taken some close-range shots of the animals as they emerged from the water. We stood together and looked northeast. The east bank was still packed solidly with caribou. It was as if they were gathering there and proceeding across in organized groups. "Now all the Ds!" Kristen called with a grin. I was counting again when she said, "Look at that one bull—he's hurt."

Among the group of animals that was picking its way out to the tip of a tiny peninsula—by then just a bare hump of icy mud completely trampled by hooves—was a big bull who could barely walk. His left shoulder was lame; he moved like a sled dog that had stove a shoulder on a downhill run of icy trail. We were spellbound as we watched him walk, head bobbing, putting almost no weight on that leg. "I wonder if he can swim?" Kristen whispered.

Slowly he made his way to the river's edge. Animals on either side of him waded into the water. He paused, head down, his antlers sweeping forward over the current. He limped in and slowly submerged all but his head and shoulders. Slowly, at half the speed of those around him, he crossed the river. As he reached shore again and could touch bottom, he almost stumbled, his head and shoulders dropping suddenly to his left as he caught himself. He stepped onto the shelf of ice, shook, and moved out of sight beneath the brow of the steep hill. I could not imagine him climbing that hill. "Wolf food, I bet." Kristen nodded. We turned back down the hill toward home, wondering aloud where the herd was leaving the cirque formed by the valley of the Hoarfrost and the high bluffs to the west.

The next day we walked up to the ridgetop that forms the cirque. The pace of the migration seemed to have slackened, but still there were caribou moving through the valley and shaking droplets of ice from their pelts. Along the high cliff over a little lake we call Obelisk there is a narrow notch like an alpine pass. Through that notch the herd was moving west. They had poured in from the east like a surging freshet of water, filled the bowl formed by the bluffs, and were spilling out through this one small cleft.

That night and the next morning three or four inches of snow fell. Two days later, on a sled with a team of five dogs, I crossed the bench where we had crouched in hiding. There was not a single track on the blanket of fresh snow. The icy ruts and trampled pathways were hidden. It was as if the herd had never been there. We didn't see a caribou again for more than a week.

Each autumn is made distinct by the arrival and passage of the herd. In some years they do not appear at all. We wait and watch the hills, scan the beach across the inlet with binoculars, strain for the sound of a big group of ravens. The first snow that stays on the ground comes in mid-October. We begin to make longer runs with the dogs, north and east toward the tundra. We talk on the radio with our neighbors once or twice a week, and in every conversation there is one item never left out: "Seen any caribou?"

On a December morning at the end of one such autumn of waiting, I was out in front of the cabin chopping fish for the dogs. The bay had frozen by then, and there were a few inches of snow atop the new ice. My friend Mike was living here with me that fall; for weeks the standing joke had been for one of us to stand in front of the cabin, binoculars raised, gaze across the river mouth and ask, "Where's the beef?"

We had managed to shoot a bull caribou in late September, far up the Hoarfrost. Our hunt for moose had not been very determined that year, and we had had no success. By American Thanksgiving in late November we had worked our way through most of the caribou meat. The vegetarian recipes were coming down from the shelf, and the cheese supply was dwindling.

The dogs set up a howl, as they always do at the approach of a motor—airplane, outboard, or snowmobile. I looked out on the bay to see if there was a skidoo coming across from Reliance. Instead, there was a long black line out there. I was astonished—caribou! Hundreds of them, strung out abreast and moving north toward the homestead.

At that first glimpse I was seized by a thrill that was purely visceral. It was the thrill of abundance, and it went straight to my stomach. In that instant I shared in a watered-down modern way a fleeting semblance of what the sight of a herd could mean to a hungry camp. "Mike—out on the lake!" I heard the shovel with which he was cleaning the dog yard clatter on the frozen ground.

We grabbed guns and a camera, the camera an after-thought, and trotted out to the island at the head of our little inlet. The line of caribou was closer, and still coming. We could see individual animals. It was a mixed group—antlerless bulls, cows, yearlings, and calves.

Mike and I had killed that September caribou only after a long jog over rolling tundra and an approach on hands and knees up the lee side of a big hill. After shooting him we had worked for the rest of the afternoon packing the meat back to the canoe, and from there back to our camp. This herd advancing on us two months later was a vivid contrast. This would be not a hunt but a harvest.

We crouched in the snow behind a rock crest of the island. The sun was just breaking the southeast horizon. A broad smile seemed to be frozen to my face.

Once in Minnesota I had watched a pair of moose advance toward me up a hill, thrilled by their approach until I began to wonder if I would be stepped on. That same thought began to cross my mind as the herd marched steadily closer. The wind was calm. On they came, seventy-five yards away, fifty yards. I rose to a half-crouch and took aim at a cow. A few animals saw my head and shoulders rise from the top of the rock, and they stopped. The cow in my sights turned, broadside to me at thirty yards. I fired and she fell. I found a second cow, the herd began to turn, and some animals broke into a nervous trot. Another shot cracked and the second cow went down kicking. Mike whooped, the herd began to run, and we stood up. We watched them turn up the bay and dissolve into the trees, moving on toward wherever it was they were going.

Two caribou were down. I picked up my spent cartridge. I am always happy at these moments. It is a strange elation, this elation upon having killed, and the lightness in my step as I walk toward a dying animal. The world in that moment narrows completely to this silent, timeless event: vivid red blood spilling onto cold windpacked snow; sharp knife blade;

pungent steaming contents of the stomach; tongue and heart cut out and set aside with the liver, choice bits.

This moment, a mixture of gratitude, concentration, relief, and wonder, does not have grief in it, if I am to portray it honestly. Neither does it have much thought. To think of the moment is to have it disappear; to become self-conscious breaks the spell. There is emotion, and some fumbling spirituality. None of it bears up well under inspection and discussion. Neither does it remain intact or credible if I try to force my thoughts and feelings into molds of a culture not my own.

Much has been written of the Native hunt, the Native kill, the reverence and ritual. But my own reverence and rituals seem to arise from deep within myself—ancient memories, perhaps, of ancestors in another part of the North. A friend, like me a white man fascinated by the wilderness, once asked if I set aside tobacco at the places where I killed caribou or moose. All I could say at first was "No." Hastily I added, "I don't usually have any tobacco with me... I don't smoke anymore." The factory-processed leaf from a warm southern hillside would not, I venture, instinctively strike me as a remembrance appropriate to the killing of an animal. One must be honest; I am wary of putting on facades of nativeness.

Another year, with another sudden appearance of the caribou in mid-October, there were four of us here. Tomoharu Fujimori, from Tokyo, was with us that fall, helping out with the dogs, and it was he who first sighted the herd. He came back from a morning run and announced, "Yes, I saw one caribou."

I think he was amazed by what those words set into motion. A quick gathering of gear, a walk up the hill, four animals down in the snow, the rest of the day spent skinning, butchering, and hauling home meat. The four of us, hands crimson with dried blood, holding them up for a snapshot at dusk, a smile on every face except Tomo's.

That night in the cabin he was quiet. I asked him why. He struggled with the English— "Everyone is so happy. I think the Inuit... said more thanks." I knew what he meant. To him, having seen for the first time a wild animal killed and cut up, we had seemed much too casual. Hunt, kill, butcher, carry meat. Laugh, talk, stop for tea, and pose for that picture. Still, I thought I had that day come closer to living here, to being truly joyful at the arrival of the herd. The actions once new and charged with that novelty were becoming familiar to me. I could relax and let myself cut loose with a feeling of celebration. I had still felt that elation and that intense gratitude as my knife and bloody hands opened and skinned and quartered the caribou. We had food and hides. We were happy. On with the feast!

The caribou are this land's living expression of its energy. They are the one large and relatively abundant creature able to take the sparse vegetation of this country and transform it into meat and fat. When they come, what one is most thankful for is that miraculous transformation. The deep-down ancient thrill that I feel in the glimpses of such abundance, in the gaze across a hillside teeming with movement and life, is at once spiritual and practical. There is movement and life in the face of cold and darkness; there too are meat and warm skins. In times past, there was *everything*: food, clothing, dogfood, lodges, kayaks, harnesses, snowshoes, bone tools...*life*.

As the most abundant food animals of a vast and stingy land, the caribou are hunted every day of their lives. Wolves and other predators begin to harass the calves almost as soon as they are born—up to eighty percent of a year's new offspring do not live until the next year's calving season. The wolves kill caribou whenever they can, at times exorbitantly. They do not do so easily, but with stamina, strength, and cunning. Humans in the north, and those imported from the south, hunt much more easily nowadays than the other predators.

In August the trophy hunters arrive. They fly to tent camps on the edge of the tundra for a week or so of guided daily hunts, watching bands of caribou as they pass, shooting at the bulls with the largest sets of antlers. The meat is secondary to the "racks" for these hunters; the beautiful short-haired August hides are of no value to them at all. Camouflaged, outfitted with the latest sporting goods, their paunches padded with bacon and eggs, fresh lobster and beefsteak, they are an incongruous sight as they stalk the herds. At week's end the bloody antlers, stripped of their velvet, are loaded into a Twin Otter, tagged and wrapped and flown south.

Perhaps, once mounted on the wall, those antlers help those hunters conjure up good memories of the crisp air on a tundra morning. Perhaps after a day at the desk they can look at the antlers and recall good stories, the welcome fatigue of days in the open, walking, carrying a pack, and hunting. I hope so.

In September, as the herds linger just north of the treeline, fattening and basking in the last warm days of summer, the natives mount their own mechanized forays. The object then is to fill the community freezers with meat. Twin Otters are dispatched to bring the hunters to the caribou. With much discussion a route is selected. The plane is loaded and flies north toward the barrens. A few caribou are sighted, a camping spot is chosen, and the pilot sets down. The radio antenna goes up, a round-the-clock progress report back to the community commences, and the hunters begin the age-old task of gathering meat. Tins of canned pork by-products, orange soda, salted kippers, and evaporated milk litter the places where the butchering is done.

The plane is called back, a Herculean load is put on, and the shuttle flights continue until the meat is all carried back to the freezers, or until the charter fund has run dry. The herds continue to saunter and linger on the autumn-reddened slopes, while the grizzlies and wolverines, ravens, gulls, and eagles find more windfalls of meat, guts, and hide lying in heaps along the lakeshores.

Mid-October is a threshold in the year of the caribou—the breeding season, or rut, and the crossing of the herd into forested country for the winter. These are the days when, if the caribou pass this way, our own hunt takes place. If the rut is still not underway we shoot bulls. If the rut has started or is already past, a few cows and yearlings will fill our cache. The bulls, so fat and prime in September and August, go downhill fast with the coming of breeding season. Their flesh becomes strongly musk-scented, their fat disappears as they cease feeding and turn to fighting and breed-ing, and even the tone of their muscles seems to dissipate. After the rut they look exhausted, shuffling along with heads down, as weak and used up as salmon at the end of an upstream run. It seems like a terrible con-dition in which to face the onset of a sub-Arctic winter, but those most exhausted and thin are those who have passed along their vigor and strength most prolifically.

In front of our cabin a small rock island juts out from the sand beach. In years of low water it is connected to the beach by a narrow spit, and by late autumn it is joined to the mainland by ice. It is where our wind-indicator flag hangs, and is thus a place we look out to often. One afternoon just after the big migration I have described, I caught sight of movement out there as I glanced at the flag. I moved around to the side of the house. There was a caribou out there, a small calf or yearling. Surprised, I took out the binoculars. A closer look explained the situation.

The animal was a calf, and quite a large one for that season. Its neck fur was matted with dried blood. One front leg dangled uselessly from the elbow, nearly severed there and hanging by a narrow strand of flesh. An ugly avulsion on its rear flank was crusted with dried blood and matted hair. The flesh and hide of its tail had been stripped away completely, and only a tiny stump of bare bone stuck up from its hind end.

Somehow it had survived the attack, almost certainly the work of one or more wolves, and by some amazing coincidence it had found refuge at one place where the wolves would hesitate to follow. It slowly shambled around the tiny island on its three good legs, scraping away the snow and bending painfully down to graze on a small patch of moss and grass.

I was struck, as I had been struck by the sight of the limping bull that had forded the Hoarfrost. Often in the past I have thought of wild animals as roaming a pure and benign landscape, unfettered by pain, with food in abundance, free from fear. For the caribou it is not very often so. This young calf, like tens of thousands of others born that previous spring, would not live to be a year old. In the panic of flight it had stumbled onto the island, safe from one predator but in the front yard of another. What could I do to help it? Nothing. Given a choice, what death would it prefer, or what death would I prefer for it?

I shot the calf, skinned it, fed most of it to my dogs and put some of it away in the cache. When I examined its wounds closely, I was astounded that it had lived as long as it had. I wondered what had kept the wolf from finishing its hunt. Perhaps it was only us, the sound of our dogs or the close smell of woodsmoke from the cabin during the night. Or perhaps the wolf had been a young one, too, just learning to hunt and with hundreds of calves upon which to sharpen its skills. One youngster had outsmarted the other, both of them new to the old game.

From November to February we may see caribou often, but only in small and scattered bands. Sometimes on a cold morning I drive a team of dogs into a stretch of trail hung with ribbons of steam. Off to each side of the trail are the fresh tracks of bounding caribou. In a fair exchange, they often use our trails through the woods, and we follow their well-packed paths across the open lakes. Always wary, they bed down on the lakes where they have good footing and a wide view, and move off to feed in the growth on the surrounding shoreline.

At times they are strangely oblivious to dogteams and snowmobiles. They are least afraid when they are in groups of a hundred or more animals, on open terrain and firm windpacked snow. Sometimes under those conditions one can drive right through a herd, the caribou barely stepping out of the way, the dogteam in a wound-up frenzy of excitement. By crouching down below the handlebar and cruising along on the back of the sled I have gone for miles through herds that for some reason had lingered on the barrens well into December.

In some years the caribou sweep south and west into the vicinity of Yellowknife, a city of more than 12,000 people. They crowd the thresholds of the airport, cross highways, and bring out weekend hunters for a bout of roadside shooting. If the herds fail to come the same way the following winter, a few people always remark that they must have learned a lesson. The year after that they come back, to be slaughtered in the same places again. There is no "lesson" for the caribou to learn, and nothing new about being hunted everywhere they go.

In spring the scattered bands assemble and begin to string together. Long purposeful lines of caribou appear on the ice of Great Slave, moving north and east. Each herd is named for the area it uses as a calving ground; we live in an area which is used at times by both the Beverly and the Bathurst herds. The cows, pregnant since autumn and beginning to feel their extra weight, set an ever-quickening pace toward the places where in June they will drop their young. Surviving calves from the previous year still travel with their mothers.

Weeks later groups of bulls wander diffidently down the big lake, eastbound also but in no hurry. They have by then begun to sprout their new antlers; thick velvety stubs protrude from their heads. This is the time of year when antler buyers from the Far East may surreptitiously appear in remote settlements, offering cash for fresh raw antler by the pound. "They grind those up for medicine over there," my friend Peter told me, "Puts lead in your pencil."

Kristen and I once came upon a dozen dead bulls, a few choice cuts of meat taken from each one and every antler gone. The missing antlers, the empty Spam cans, and the tracks of skidoos heading southwest told the story. We spent the rest of the bright May night hauling home load after load of meat on a big komatik sled.

By late June there are no barrenland caribou around Great Slave. So I thought until on a canoe trip early one July a yearling stepped out of the forest near George Back's old Fort Reliance. There are a few stragglers left behind, evidently, and some groups may get cut off by spring breakup and spend the summer in the forest, never joining the herds on the barrens.

The calves are born in distant places which strategically put them beyond the range of many wolves, who must themselves attend to the making of a den for the May whelping of their own young. The caribou join in tremendous groups shortly after calving. By that time, the month of July, they are a motley bunch. Their thick winter hair is bleached near-ly white, and it falls off in big patches; they are tormented incessantly by clouds of mosquitoes, warble flies, and blackflies.

If there is a time of year when caribou find a breath of peace, though, it must be early August. The barrens are a lush green; already a few cold nights have put down the hordes of insects, and the feeding is restfully easy on breezy tundra slopes. During this brief respite the caribou, espe-cially the big males, put on a thick layer of body fat in preparation for the coming swing south and the autumn rut.

I have written myself into a trap, describing this storybook "year of the caribou" as if the caribou were predictable and abundant, as if the land was teeming with them and not instead barren, austere, and desert-ed. It is a trap laid by the television series "Nature Documentaries," by Walt Disney and Marlin Perkins, by canoeists who venture down an arc-tic river in summer and return south to proclaim "the barrenlands" a mis-nomer. The land, they say, is rich with life of every kind.

The Barrenlands is no misnomer, for at least eight or nine months out of every year. The fact that this landscape should be acclaimed as being so full of wildlife only tells how thoroughly decimated and mono-cultural many landscapes to the south have become, and how blind most people are to the wildlife that thrives there yet. The explorers who coined the term "barrenlands" reached those lands after weeks and months of travel through wild country more hospitable, rich, and diverse. There are more whitetail deer *killed* by hunters and highway traffic in the states of Wisconsin and Minnesota *each year* than there are caribou alive in any of the largest herds in the Arctic—the Porcupine herd, the Bathurst herd, or the Beverly herd.

There are not many caribou. A given patch of the landscape that is their home range is almost always devoid of them. To see caribou in a huge herd, to glimpse *la foule*, is exceptional and thus memorable. It is not a pre-dictable annual event.

In 1980 and 1981 I travelled for six weeks each spring, by dogteam across 1,400 miles of caribou range in the Northwest Territories—the Keewatin, the Thelon watershed, Great Slave Lake. I never saw a caribou. In 1983 I made a canoe trip east from Pike's Portage and up to Artillery Lake in August and September, intent on breaking the jinx and finally running into the caribou. Nothing. At last, toward the end of that sum-mer, the fellow who is now my neighbor gave me a ride a hundred miles north of Great Slave in his airplane, and after much searching we finally

30

spotted a few scattered groups of caribou, not more than a dozen in any one place.

Over the past two summers I have logged more than 100,000 miles of flight north and east of Yellowknife, mostly over tundra and at low altitudes. Once in all those miles have I chanced to overlook a herd that was streaming along like those herds on the television programs. A solid swath of caribou over a mile and a half wide, more than eight miles long, rushed headlong down the west side of the Back River one evening in late July. The pilot with whom I was flying, Mike Murphy, has flown low over the tundra like that for ten years, a couple of million miles, and he was shaking his head that night, saying he'd never seen a herd like *that*. It was a thrilling sight, even through a quarter-inch of plexiglass at 150 miles an hour. I will never forget it. What is sometimes forgotten, or never told, is just how rare that sight is; how lucky one is to stumble upon such a spectacle.

This year is shaping up to be one of those quiet ones. It is early November and there are no caribou around the lower Hoarfrost. Trappers on the radio are asking each other twice a day if anyone has spotted any. Convinced that this will be a lean season, many trappers have not even ventured out to their autumn camps. No one knows where the caribou are. Where in the world do half a million animals go?

I enjoy this uncertainty, the mystery of the caribou. Of course I can say that this year, with a bull moose and a fat young bear hanging in our meat cache, to go along with a year's supply of store-bought groceries on shelves in the cabin's back room. The missing caribou of this and other years heighten my appreciation for the true character of this land, its harshness and unpredictability. And when they arrive, if they do, we will greet them again with wonder—where did they come from? Where will they go?

From my diary: "October 11, 1992. Yesterday the ravens told us in the morning, flying out of the east in the first light. Kristen counted 23 as she paused between the small cabin and the main one. It could only mean one thing, really—caribou. We fed the dogs and did the chores; brought binoculars, camera, rifle, and a pup; and headed for the high bluff behind us. Immediately north of the homestead we began to see scattered tracks in the light dusting of snow. The migration? Perhaps not. But then as we climbed we saw whole pathways trampled in the snow, places where dozens of animals had passed. Still we saw no movement, only the ravens flapping and croaking overhead. We topped the bluff and the dramatic view of the valley of the Hoarfrost lay beneath us. Kristen saw them first, and I spotted them then myself—a file of animals moving west across 'the meadow,' a grassy swale below Obelisk Lake.

"We found a vantage point and settled in with binoculars to piece the story together. Clearly this *was* the migration which we have so blithely come to expect each October. The herd was westbound and the bulls were not yet in rut. We made a plan and split up at the fork of the Lacy Pond trail. I would shoot five bulls if I could, in as accessible a place as possible, and Kristen would go with her camera to Lacy Pond and spend the day taking photographs—the bright light and the passage of animals near the falls was too good to pass up.

"This morning we are awake in the dark, drinking coffee and writing in our journals. We will walk up the hill to where the gutted, headless carcasses of four bull caribou lie in the marsh grass, frosted but not frozen in this Indian Summer weather.

"Time for breakfast, fuel for the day. I eat the strong smooth muscle of a bull caribou's heart, and wonder about the one I wounded, the one that ran off carrying my bullet in his shoulder, the one I could not find in the twilight. He probably is not seeing this morning, or maybe he sees it through a haze of pain and shock, lying alone in some hollow among the stunted spruce, with a flock of ravens circling above him."

OLD BLAZES

There are signs, there are stories, and there is imagination. When I spent the summer of 1983 camped down the bay, alone much of the time with my ten dogs, I repeatedly conjured up an illusion. It was quite real, and I let myself indulge in it. I would see, usually in the obliquely angled light of late evening, a small bent figure watching me from the crest of a rock island, or peering out through the spruces on the shoreline. Imagination filled in details: his face was wrinkled, darkened and pinched by years of frost, smoke, sun, and hunger; his clothes were worn skins, dirty cotton, and ragged wool; puckered moosehide moccasins were on his feet; his hair was thin and white. Old timer, boy.

He is the old one, one I've not had here. Alaska poet John Haines had old Fred Campbell and others, his neighbors in Alaska when he first arrived to homestead along the Tanana. Back in northern Minnesota I knew several old-timers, among them Bill Magie, who'd been around "since Christ was a cowboy," guiding, surveying, flying, and mining. Bill's stories and his detailed memory of that land and its lakes filled in blanks in my own geography; knowing him helped me to better and

33

more quickly come to know the country.

Here it has been different. In the late seventies the grand old man of Reliance, Gus D'Aoust, went away for good, his eyesight failing and his knee joints giving out after more than fifty years of trapping, trading, and hunting. He was gone before I arrived.

Louison Drybones was the last of the Chippewayan barrenland trappers to depend on a dogteam. Late in that summer of 1983 I had a fleeting opportunity to join him, to go out to his trapping grounds as his green sidekick and spend the autumn with him at Williams Lake. He wanted a partner, being in his seventies then and having had a colostomy, and none of the native fellows from Snowdrift were inclined to join him. But I called Minnesota from the radiotelephone station in Reliance and was told that I still had a job waiting for me. I went dutifully south at the start of September and I never met Louison, who, like Gus, had died by the time I moved to the Territories. I will always muse over that lost opportunity, and wonder what insights and lessons I might have gleaned in that remote autumn.

The peers of Louison and Gus are gone as well. The younger natives that pass this way now come roaring through, always bound somewhere in a rush, astride gleaming skidoos or hurtling down the lake pushed by the latest outboards. A bit baffled by our ongoing efforts here, they stop by to borrow something or to spend the night. Their elders have all moved to town, taking their memories and knowledge with them.

I talk with my handful of non-native cohorts, but not one of us living out here is over fifty years old, and we are all from somewhere else. All that we have seen for ourselves is the latest drawn-out decline of what has gone on here. This has been a land of transient lives, of boom and bust, of forays and temporary establishments. I find myself adopting the local parlance and referring to our home here as our camp, as if tomorrow or the day after we might pull it all down, pack it up, and head off. The canoe that hangs on the back wall of the little cabin seems to announce that possibility.

I crave a history. I want to weave myself and my own story into the ongoing terse narrative of this place, a narrative I can only dimly discern. I hungrily gather whatever fragments, glimpses, and signs I can find, in order to patch together a backdrop for my own years here.

The country is full of vague leavings. Old camps in ruins, traps hung in trees, rock cairns on tundra hilltops, the ancient remains of a bark canoe in the moss alongside a secluded cove. Old axe-cuts or blazes on spruce trunks lead up small drainages or outline the perimeters of some forgotten prospector's claims. Crystalline sap, brittle and bitter, is congealed over the old wounds in the bark. I wander the hills and try to flesh out old splinters of bone, metal, and wood. I circle my plane over the twisted wreckage of a by-gone crash. I rummage through the archives and read the words of Hearne, Seton, Pike, Anderson, and Ingstad.

Things surface. Out feeding the dogs one summer night, I found a trade-axe head, crudely cast and crimped in an archaic style at least 150 years old. Esker had uncovered it as she dug a cool place to lie in the moist sand. Her burrow was almost two feet deep, and the small axe-head lay on top of her pile of diggings. On the wall in the kitchen hangs a weathered paddle blade, cedar and narrow in the style of the fur-trade voyageurs. It too I found in the sand on the beach here. Up the hill beyond our cabin is an old grave, a small rectangle sunk into the ground, with shards of carefully carved spruce along its outline. A native child must be buried there.

The climate here, a cold desert, acts as if to belie the dearth of human endeavors. Remnants decay so slowly that they bolster a sense of timelessness. The main events in recorded history, the main characters and their doings, are referred to offhandedly, as if at any moment they might resume, or reappear. "Back went that way on his trip," say my neighbors, who stop short of referring to Captain Back as George, but still manage to sound chummy with the men on the British expedition of 1833 to 1835. It is the same even with reference to Samuel Hearne, who walked through this region en route to and from the Coppermine River in 1772; it is especially so with the white-fox trappers of the 1920s and 1930s.

As if to strengthen this impression that the past is hermetically preserved here, a team of archaeologists and stonemasons camped out at the site of the original Fort Reliance in the summer of 1987, and spent a few weeks refurbishing the crumbling hearths that had heated the winter quarters of Back's expedition. The workers installed a plaque and laid out a log-bordered walkway from the steep shoreline to the three renovated columns of stone and clay. Back's Chimneys were restored, and now look like restorations. The aura of a little theme park pervades the clearing where they stand. I half-expect an interpreter in period garb to step from the brush and deliver his spiel.

I think it would have been better, both more dramatic and more honest, if the chimneys had been allowed to continue their slow crumbling— to actually *become* 160 years old, and 200, 400, and dust.

I have a strong interest in George Back and his journey. He camped here the night before he and his crew began their "toilsome Ascent of Hoar Frost River." Like many explorers he was class-conscious, arrogant, and a quintessential racist. He was also a leader respected and liked by his men, a careful planner, a bit of a dandy, and an expert at getting to and from the most remote reaches of North America. Again and again he proved his proficiency by leading his crews home safely against tremendous odds.

Back left London in February of 1833 to lead a small expedition to the Arctic Coast. He was to proceed north from the watershed of the Mackenzie River to an unexplored river that the Chipewyan Indians called Thleweechodezeth—The Great Fish River, now named the Back. Back's purposes were to explore and map the regions he traversed, and to search for *another* British expedition—a naval reconnaissance of the Arctic Ocean led by Captain James Ross. By the autumn of 1832 Ross was overdue; he had not been heard from and was presumed to be in trouble. In a small-scale rehearsal for the various Franklin searches twenty years later, Back set off over a new route to the unmapped coast of the Arctic Ocean, to search for a lone ship, its crew, or its wreckage. As it turned out, Ross was safely back in England before Back set off down the Great Fish River. Back was advised of this by a letter which reached Fort Reliance in April, but his sponsors directed him to proceed with his plans in the interest of exploration.

He assembled a mixed crew of soldiers, voyageurs, Indian guides, and a fellow gentleman, Dr. Richard King, as he made his way north and west by the canoe routes of the fur trade during the spring and summer of 1833. Arriving at Fort Resolution, the established jumping-off place for the Mackenzie watershed, he divided his party and set off with one canoe for the northeast tip of Great Slave Lake. Summer was passing, and all he could hope to do before winter was to locate the headwaters of the Thleweecho, while a Mr. R. McLeod of the Hudson Bay Company took charge of building a winter quarters down on the big lake.

On August 18, 1833, Back could see the hills at the eastern end of Great Slave Lake rising ahead of him. He was about to give orders for the canoes to steer for the head of the lake, "when, launching past some rocks, which had shut out the land in their direction, we opened suddenly on a small bay, at the bottom of which was seen a splendid fall... It was the object of our search—the river we were to ascend; so, without noticing the very significant gestures of my crew, indicating the impossibility of ascending it, I immediately landed, and set them about drying and thoroughly repairing the small canoe..."

Back was here, at the mouth of "Hoar Frost River." I can walk out the door of our cabin and look across at his campsite on the east side of the inlet. In fact, most of the logs in these walls came from that level grove over there, and certainly some of the big trees were more than 160 years old when I came striding up to them with my chainsaw. I cut them down, rafted them over to our acre of beach, peeled, fitted and scribed them. I now sleep and write within a snug square of trees that were too young and green to get tossed onto George's campfire that night, as he wrote up his journal and recorded the observations he had made with his sextant, his latitude in error by just two-thirds of a nautical mile.

At the close of a two-day journey, the speed of which I find astonishing, Back and his men were camped on Cook Lake, twenty-five miles of "appalling cascades and rapids" above the river mouth. From there they went north, crossed two heights of land, located the headwaters of the Thleweechodezeth, and on September 7 arrived back on Great Slave Lake to overwinter and prepare for the next summer's journey. Those fellows could travel.

When I study Back's description of his journey, his narrative makes his movements and encampments so plain that it is tempting to search for signs of them. But a small party of men in a bark canoe, with a load "consisting of three bags of pemmican, with a little ammunition, tobacco, & c." does not leave very much that can be found a century and a half later. Still, we keep looking.

Several years ago Kristen and I spent an entire autumn day on the first calm reach of the Hoarfrost above its outlet, a three-mile length of river less than a hundred yards wide. Here Back and his men had made their first night's camp at a rare "level spot on which to pitch the tent." We scoured the banks of the river, tried to imagine how the scene might have looked and what might have changed. We found two old campsites, one of them from ten or twelve years earlier, and the other—dated by counting the rings on the branch of a spruce that had been partially cut for firewood—fifty or sixty years old. Of course, I told myself, at a brief overnight stop like that nothing large and durable was likely to have been left behind. Back's may be the last documented canoe journey up "this turbulent and unfriendly river," and this climate may be an effective preservative, but 160 years is still a long time.

A rusted thermos bottle sits on my desk, just behind the typewriter. The lines engraved on its tarnished baseplate read: "Stanley Super-Vac.

Patented in U.S.A. Sept. 12, 23." Around the perimeter of the base are specific instructions "FOR HOT LIQUIDS, FOR COLD LIQUIDS," and "AFTER USING." Dead center, set apart in cursive type and quotation marks, is the clincher: "It will not break."

So the thermos bottle was still a recent innovation in the gear of Gene Olson and Emil Bode (Bo-dee) during the summer of 1930. I can see them hunkered down on the lee side of a tarpaulin or a toboggan, heaping praise on the Stanley Super-Vac in their bouncing Swedish accents, marvelling at a hot cup of coffee without the need to gather twigs for a midday fire.

Over a hundred miles east of our homestead that thermos lay in a mat of moss and grass about forty feet north of the remains of Bode and Olson's final camp. A hundred yards away lie their skeletons and the wooden nameplates of their shared grave. Sometime during those years the chrome-plated cup that covers the cork in the bottle was dented by small teeth, perhaps those of a fox. The cork was in place when I came across the thermos, and the bottle had a little water in it.

"They had been in partnership for some time and had been successful. For some time they had been established in a tent close to a small clump of trees..." reads the *1932 Commissioner's Report* from the Royal Canadian Mounted Police, "All their arrangements bespoke comfort."

All their arrangements bespoke comfort. Meat grinder, pressurized gas lamp, the framework of a tent at least ten by fourteen feet, which they had insulated with dozens of thick caribou hides. An ample sheetmetal stove, a sturdy sawbuck, a whetstone. Comfort, pride, efficiency.

And up the hill lie the two men's bones, each skull smashed in, preserved in a cairn of logs and boulders. The police patrol, forming a makeshift coroner's jury, hastily built that grave on a bitter day in January 1932. A few weeks later another Swedish immigrant, Otto "Blacky" Lanner, shot himself in the head. A year had passed since the two murders. Lanner, a former partner of Emil Bode, had been questioned by the police. As he lay dying he muttered the names of Bode and Olson. At his hellish, decrepit shack on Timber Bay of Artillery Lake, Lanner left a note in Swedish, which the police translated for the record: "Don't ever live alone it is the most dangerous thing there is. And trust in God and do all things well. I am a great sinner and don't want to live any longer." Prior to this his diary read "Cold West Wind" for fifteen days straight.

There is a realm of the past that is beyond my empathy. When I stand at the stones of a native tent ring or at the posts surrounding a

Chipewyan grave, or when I find a stone arrowhead on the crest of an esker, all of my efforts to visualize the people who made these things, to put myself in their place and imagine their world—seem contrived and academic, and I fail. The paths of our cultures diverged long ago, and I can't find in my gut the *feeling* of those lives. I can think about them, and quicken at times to those thoughts, but I can't get them inside of me.

But when I stood on a hot July day on that hilltop alongside the last camp of those two Swedes and held in my hand the slice of wooden grave marker with "OLSON" carved in it, I felt the spirit of those men and the span of years between us in a way that no native tent ring or arrowhead has ever brought. The letters of their names, what little I knew of their lives and work, tools like the thermos and meat grinder lying in the wreckage of their camp, all linked them to me and to the start of the changes that have characterized this country over the past seventy years. They were immigrants to Canada, searching and learning the landscape, revelling in its vastness and freedom, studying and adopting the old ways of the North. But they were bringing new tools and techniques, and were driven by new motives and a changing, distant economy.

The late 1920s and early 1930s were the start of a new era in the North. The Depression left much of the continent destitute, but fur prices were extraordinary. A winter's take of white-fox pelts was worth a small fortune. The airplane had begun to change the world completely, but men like Bode and Olson still went to their trapping ground by canoe in late summer, packing woodstove and nails and gas lamp and bullets over portage after portage, to some new country north and east of Great Slave.

With them they carried tiny bottles of strychnine sulfate. They were ruthlessly practical men, hard-bitten Swedes, Norwegians, Germans, and Scots. A box of small metal traps weighed fifteen pounds, whereas a single pound of strychnine could kill many dozens of foxes, wolves, wolverines, and marten.

The winter camps of the white-fox trappers were scattered across the tundra for thousands of miles, in a great sweeping curve southeast from Inuvik to Churchill. The camp of Bode and Olson sits more than a hundred miles east of Reliance, in a blank stretch of tundra near the lakes now named for the two. It seems to me to be an odd place for a pair of experienced trappers to have made camp for a two-year stint on the Barrens.

But what do I know, across these sixty-some years? What do I know about those two dead Swedes, earlier arrivals on this wild edge of Canada? How can I write about them with any credibility, my typewriter clack-

clacking beneath the twelve-volt fluorescent bulb, the sun just lighting the beach where Emil Bode, Gene Olson, Al Greathouse, Blacky Lanner, Price, Hornby, Mackay, and all the others would have camped on their way down McLeod Bay? What can I say about them?

Only that I think I can sometimes catch a tantalizing glimpse of their lives. I feel vaguely connected to them. There have been only a few dozen of us immigrants, each of us wrapped in our own times, who have wandered this amazing silence and distance, watched for blazes and cairns, wondered who was here before us and what their days and years were like.

To move through a wild land and know nothing of its human history would be an impoverishment. An understanding of the past enables a clearer appreciation of the present. In a time of rapid change, historical perspective can help to place that change in context. I gain a fresh outlook on the present whenever I deliberately set out to do something the old, outmoded way—to sail a canoe, to steam and bend a wooden dogsled runner, to read a sextant, to make a basket from birchbark or a fire without matches.

In learning such archaic skills, in looking back, one must be careful. That historical perspective, especially in the wilderness and along a frontier, can all too easily become a fuzzy and simplistic nostalgia. Like any rigid doctrine, a blind belief that the old ways were better, that other times and people were better, is shallow. To think that one was "born too late," that one's own culture is completely trivialized, polluted, and destructive, provides no clear vision and slim hope of happiness. Tempting as that line of thinking may be, it does not lead to the lesson I am trying to learn from old blazes, from history. I want to move forward down the trail, even blaze new trails, but I want to keep clear the view back over my shoulder, to remember where I came from, and to learn what journeys through this place have been like for others.

As seasons pass, the history of this place includes us, whether or not we take notice of or strive for that inclusion. The blazes we see up in the countless small drainages north and east of here are now more likely to be our own than anyone else's. We skim our own history as the dogs tow us along a familiar trail: there's where I got that damned skidoo bogged down in slush and nearly froze my toes; there's where we camped and saw the musk-ox tracks; that flat is where the cabin logs came from. I have a rare chance to date precisely the signs of a people's activities on the land—here's what a blaze on a spruce trunk looks like after a year, after three, after seven... I know exactly how old those blazes are, because I cut them.

I have not seen the old one lately. My first years here have been a flurry of work and activity, with most of my days dominated by immediate concerns and preoccupations. I have drifted, I think inevitably, from the contemplative and receptive frame of mind which, in that initial summer of exploration, helped me to conjure the old timer's image.

Perhaps—and this is my hope these years—I can over time circle back to that more receptive and visionary stance. If I do, I trust that my glimpses of the old one will revive. The sight of him will then be more empathetic, more understanding and appreciative, than those first encounters. I will have tasted by then some parallels to his own seasons in the North: hard and easy years, weeks and months both lean and plentiful. I might even by then have gained some measure of respect in his wizened gaze.

Given even more time—decades, a lifetime—my own doings here, my flesh and bone, kin and offspring may meld with the land. In some distant year I may peer out from the shadows myself. Some lingering part of me may watch, bemused and a bit skeptical, as some starry-eyed new arrival cuts a first tentative blaze into the bark of a spruce tree.

41

THE MEMORY OF SMELL

I am behind our cabin late on an October afternoon, chopping open the skinned head of a cow moose. The head is centered between my feet, lying on the packed snow. I turn it slightly to position it for the next blow, and raise the axe. The nose points back toward me, a small patch of brown hair still attached where I did not bother to skin out the intricate infoldings and curves of the nostrils. This trail axe I am using is sharp but not very heavy. In a swift smooth motion I bring it up, swing it overhead and drive it down hard into the forehead bone between the eye sockets. The bit drives through the quarter-inch thick skull and on into the soft pale brain.

This is what I am after, this brain. Two more blows at cross angles and I can lift away a rhombus-shaped plate of skull. The edges of the hole are jagged and sharp. They cut my cold fingers as I lift the shattered bone. Now I can scoop, tearing the chilled mass of the brain free from its membrane, smushing it like half-frozen porridge between my numbing fingers. It is a yellow-gray palmful, wrinkled and convoluted, laced with tiny red blood vessels. Another pocket of brain tissue lies

43

deep down and back, low toward where the spinal cord gathers and starts off down the neck. I dig hard with my index finger for this and lift it out in small chunks.

The brain is so small, a mere dollop of delicate flesh encased in the giant head. This moose weighed over 500 pounds. A caribou brain—the caribou an animal one-fourth that size—is just as big.

My friend Ed is nearby, half-watching what I do as he finishes a repair to a dogsled. There is a lively blaze of spruce burning in a cut-off barrel top, heating an enormous pot of meat scraps and bones. As evening comes on we have both moved our work into the flickering firelight. I turn to him, holding out the brain of the cow moose. "Guess it takes more brains to be a caribou than it does to be a moose." He chuckles.

Yes, I think, in a way it makes sense. Annual migrations over many hundreds of miles (which caribou make and moose do not) and adaptation to life in both forest and tundra—maybe that takes more thought, more storage of information, than the local life of a moose. Or perhaps, like us, neither animal utilizes anywhere near the full capacity of its brain; we all get along on some small fraction of the lumps we carry inside our skulls.

It is late October, and getting dark, and I am getting cold. I stand with a half-frozen moose brain in one hand and in the other hand my axe, its handle red with dried and frozen blood—stand for just a moment thinking of thought and life, a brain and a moose. I long to let my mind work its way along this theme for a while, to talk to Ed and warm up by the fire, but there is more work to do. Autumn here is a slim season for reverie.

I drop the moose brain into a big tin can that already holds three caribou brains and the brain of another moose. I set the can just inside the tent we are using for storage. The brains can freeze over winter. I will use them in the spring.

I use these brains for tanning. Boil them in water, melt three pounds of lard and a couple of cups of shaved soap, and stir it all together. Slather this greasy, lumpy mixture onto the flesh side of a scraped moose skin. Heat the hide gently by stretching it on a wooden frame and tilting it toward a slow fire, until the grease and brain and soap move through the skin and splotch it with translucent grease marks. This tans the skin. Some chemical in the brain tissue is vital to the process. The brain-lard-soap treatment is one of seven steps which together transform a raw moose skin, one side thick with dark coarse hair, the other slippery with blood and dangling chunks of meat and fat, into a light, supple, smoky-smelling eight foot square of tanned moosehide.

There is no boot or shoe as warm and practical in deep dry cold as moosehide mukluks lined with caribou-hair insoles. With knee-high uppers of the stiff white canvas that is used to cover traditional canoes, and lined with two thick layers of heavy wool, the mukluk is light, warm, and easily dismantled to dry at the end of the day. The smoke-tanned moosehide has an insulating value far superior to store-bought leather. At forty or fifty degrees below zero, I know what I want on my feet.

The cost, in money, of such mukluks or moccasins is next to nothing. A few dollars for lard and soap and bullets, maybe ten dollars worth of canvas and thread. The cost, as in so many old ways of doing things, is in time: days of hunting, hours of messy fleshing with a long tool cut from the foreleg bone of a moose, more hours scraping with a steel scraper made from an old file heated red over a stove burner... days of soaking and wringing the hide, rinsing it, stretching it, drying and delicately smoking it. All told this is a week or more of work. Then there are the long evenings spent sewing the thick hide, shaping it to the foot, adding canvas and laces and trim. Finally, I have my moosehide mukluks. If time were money, which it is not, I could never afford such luxurious footwear.

Last spring we had a fellow here, a participant on a dogsledding trip, a brilliant man who was taking a break from his work in a neurobiology laboratory at the University of Wisconsin. His name was Evan Kanter. One morning Evan was splitting kindling for the cabin stove. He turned to me with a smile and said, "I've decided that chopping wood beats chopping brains."

He told me that part of his lab work involved slicing certain portions of the brains of rats into wafer-thin cross-sections. Floated in various ionic solutions, these cross-sections were then "excited" with tiny surges of electrical current. He was studying the region of the brain that had to do with the sense of smell, the most simple of the senses. He was trying to understand the mechanism of the memory of smells—how, biochemically, a rat remembered smells. This could, he thought, lead to further understanding of other mechanisms of memory.

These moose and caribou must have been able to remember smells. Having smelled wolf, or smoke, or male or female, they must have been able to call up this stored smell-memory and use it again—to trigger wariness, or to rendezvous with an old broad-antlered bull, as the cow moose had in a marsh at dawn on a cold October morning. I shot both moose that morning, filling our annual household quota of two moose. I smelled the bull from ten yards back as I walked up to skin and butcher him. He reeked with a pungent scent like old strong urine, the powerful aroma of breeding season.

So, somehow, in the small pocket of brain tissue down low at the base of the bone-armoured cavity I had opened with my axe, the cow moose had stored her memory of that smell of bull. It was an odor that she had certainly smelled before and remembered, for she had borne a calf in the previous spring; her udders still contained a splash of milk.

My hands are cold. Skinning heads and chopping brains is hard work, Evan. Hard cold messy work that people have been doing for thousands and thousands of years. Ashes and urine provided other tanning chemicals in centuries before pork lard and detergent flakes, but the brains have always been a necessary additive. All across the north this method has been used to tan hides—whitetail, moose, caribou. The people who perfected it are not my people, but I am learning. There are holes worn in the toes of my old mukluks; by next year I will need another pair.

Ed walks past me, hauling the finished sled, heading inside to warm up and happy to be done for the day. I chop the moose head in half just below the eyes, chop the jaws and nose away so that the pieces,—bone, meat, and all—will fit into the boiling barrel. I drop the two heavy chunks of head into the soup, adding their rich muscle and fat, the tissue of lips, nostrils, eyes and upper neck. A cloud of steam rises into the cold air. The barrel is full to the brim now with the two moose heads, three caribou heads, and thirty or forty pounds of meat from the sections of hide I've already fleshed. It will make an excellent broth for our thirty sled dogs, who will enjoy licking the bones absolutely clean over the next few days. I warm my aching fingers in the steam above the barrel, wash my hands briskly with some clean snow, warm and dry them again in the heat. I sink the axe into a big log. It is dark now, and I'm glad to be done with this task.

The fire crackles and flares. The broth and smoke smell good together. I remember that smell perfectly—from last year, and from other years, and from farther back than that.

DHC-6

I am a bundle of contradictions.

I like the smell of a spruce campfire in the morning, the quiet lapping of water on a crescent-shaped beach, the steady leverage of my arms and back sent along the shaft of a canoe paddle, the silent trot of a dogteam in fresh snow. I like the steadfast trustworthiness of hand tools—claw hammer, rip saw, brace, and auger. I like the way a sail bellies with wind, and the firm ache in my calves as I hump a load over a portage. I like to run, gulping lungfulls of clean cool air. The movements of life, silent and direct, are beautiful.

I like too the smooth advance of the paired power levers of a 300-series DeHavilland Twin Otter, the spine-shaking thunder of two Pratt and Whitney turbine engines as they spin screaming propeller blades in full fine pitch. I like the ponderous heft of the control yoke pulled back in my lap as we start the takeoff run, the gentle nosing forward as the massive floats rise onto their steps, the glance at the torque gauges pegged on the redlines, and the temperature needles as they climb through 675 degrees Celsius. Airspeed 60 knots. A gentle tug on the yoke. Airborne. Beautiful.

47

There are machines which embody any frontier, being both a product of civilization and a vital tool for its encounter with wilderness. I think of those trains that run north to Hudson Bay at Churchill, and still stop at a certain milepost to let off or take on a trapper, a canoe, six dogs, and three packsacks. The notion that a train still makes such stops is a comfort to me.

For me, the twin-engined bushplanes called Twin Otters are those trains. I first encountered these planes before I became a pilot, while making a dogteam trip from Yellowknife to the Thelon River in 1981. A rush was on for uranium then, and the mineral prospects were in the sandstones beneath the Thelon watershed 130 miles east of Reliance.

A pilot named Len Robinson, who still flies Twin Otters in the outback anywhere from Burma to Greenland, was hauling fuel supplies to the staking camps that spring. Three round-trips out from Yellowknife to the upper Thelon River on some days, at about 600 miles a trip—"I just strap my ass in this seat and stay there," he told me. When putting out caches of fuel drums in winter, a Twin Otter never stops moving. The landing on a frozen lake is followed by a slow forward taxi over the snow-covered tundra. The cargo door is opened and the co-pilot kicks the sealed drums out one at a time, leaving a line of them beside the ski tracks in the snow. The door is closed, the engines spool up, and the plane lifts off.

Len took an interest in our dogteam journey, and offered to cache some supplies for us along the route. He did more than that. I remember hearing the drone of his engines over our camp one evening, miles from his direct route home, watching him circle, tilt his wings once, and disappear into the west: "Just wanted to see where youse were." And once more, far out on the Thelon, at a placed called Warden's Grove, he again diverted to check on our progress. He landed that time, and advised us with a smile that should we run low on food for our dogs, "The Queen wouldn't miss a few caribou." We were law-abiding foreigners in the midst of the Thelon Game Sanctuary, but he was doing his best to enlighten us. When two of us with ten dogs wound up back in Reliance, it was Len again in the Twin Otter, C-GMAS, who lifted us all back to Yellowknife. By then I was convinced, and a year later I got my pilot's license.

Flying added a new layer to my perception of the North. The view from 3,000 feet above familiar lakes and trails in the Boundary Waters forever changed and enhanced my understanding of that country. Idealist that I am, I wrestled with the notion of taking on this mechanical set of wings, of burning that fuel, of shortcutting time and distance. My entrenched and naive notions evolved; I began to see beauty in engines and engineering, in aluminum fuselages, in asphalt runways bordered by automated lights. And always at the back of my mind was the image of Len and that Twin Otter on skis, a craftsman and a craft linked to my earliest adventures in the far north.

When I took some pilot training in a Twin Otter eleven years after first seeing one, my instructor remarked that he considered the PT6A-27 turboprop engine to be "an *elegant* piece of machinery." That description struck me because I have always used the word "elegance" in an unorthodox way, with reference to simple tools and silent, archaic modes of transportation. A sharp handsaw is elegant. A canoe in whitewater, paddled with grace, is elegant. A sixteen-dog team moving swiftly up a steep hill is elegant. To my mind, a perfect match of form, function, and efficiency deliver elegance. How could those engines slung beneath those massive metal wings, thrumming at a deafening pitch, igniting 600 pounds of jet fuel every hour, embody elegance?

I've been won over now. I discern and appreciate that elegance. Those engines are utterly reliable, *elegant* combinations of form, function, power, and efficiency. The work that they accomplish, when fitted to the frame of a Twin Otter and dispatched across the formidable distances of the North, is astonishing.

The designated initials for the Twin Otter are DHC-6, standing for DeHavilland Corporation, model 6. A friend of mine, faced with the need to move dogs and equipment to the far west end of Great Slave Lake, in springtime with uncertain ice and snow conditions, remarked that such northern logistics could prove overwhelming. Peter Arychuk, who manages a fleet of four Twin Otters for hire in Yellowknife, smiled: "You only have to know the magic word—DHC-6!"

The Twin Otter, fitted with floats or skis or oversized tires, is the workhorse of the North. That is a tired metaphor, but I'll trot it out again. Like a workhorse, a well-worn Twin Otter is neither sleek nor luxurious. The interior of the cargo area, where the passenger seats fold down from the sidewalls, is as plush as the bed of a gravel truck. The seats are cramped, the corrugated metal floor is scratched and stained, and a sturdy ladder bolted in place leads down from the cargo door to a patched pontoon. Airsickness bags and life jackets are stored above the seats; an axe and some survival gear are crammed in the tail along with a kerosene-soaked set of refuelling hoses.

One load coming back from a tundra camp might consist of a ton or more of greasy drill rods, a dozen empty fuel drums, and twenty leaking plastic sacks of foul-smelling garbage. The next load, already milling around on the dock as the plane is tied up, might be a party of lawyers and a judge heading for a small settlement to hold court. A quick mop goes over the floor, fuel hoses refill the beast's enormous belly tanks, seats are folded down and snapped in place, and the three-piece suits climb aboard. Frills and affectations may just as well stay home, or go back south.

Midnight, June 20, 1992. I am northeastbound from Yellowknife at 7,500 feet above sea level, about 6,000 feet above the boulders, lakes, and dwindling patches of forest visible through breaks in the clouds. I am perched in the right seat of Twin Otter C-GNPS. Blair Morphet is the captain; he is flying the airplane. The sun is down but the northern horizon is bright, and at this season there is no darkness. We are bound for Esker Lake, a small prospecting camp where half a dozen people are gearing up for the summer's work. One of them, Vic Waugh, is about to become a father. His wife is in labor at the hospital in Yellowknife, and our goal for the night is to bring Vic back to join her. Five propane cylinders and a huge stack of plywood are on board to make up our outbound load. The oblong screen of the navigation computer is lit with the terse details of our position, heading and speed: TO ESKER 124 NM :54 TK 016 GS 142 kt.

Tonight, as a rookie co-pilot, I am flying along more as a glorified stevedore than as any vital part of the flight crew. Strictly speaking, a Twin Otter does not require two pilots. The co-pilot may increase the safety and efficiency of the flights, but some captains at times make it plain that they would really rather be alone. "We're going to replace all the co-pilots," the saying goes, "by putting a big rock in the right seat of the cockpit and putting a pair of sunglasses on the rock."

An hour and a half out of Yellowknife, Blair throttles back and we begin our descent. The cloud layer below us is nearly solid; we drop through a ragged hole and emerge less than 300 feet above rain-soaked drab tundra. We run through the Descent checklist: altimeters, hydraulics, position report, approach briefing. Flaps, props, and lights will be set on our final approach. "Nice down here," Blair mutters. "Windy."

Esker Lake has a bad reputation. There have been two serious accidents there in recent years: one a crash of a Twin Otter. The low ceiling, gusty wind, and rain driving down in sheets will make for a difficult landing. The computer reads down the distance remaining and our speed, then flashes a new message: "Arrival at ESKER in 60 seconds... 59... 58..." I peer ahead. It is nearly one in the morning, and beneath the solid overcast the light is dim. We are still at cruise speed, and the tundra whips by below us.

I spot a cluster of white tents set at the foot of a low ridge. The ridge is a glacial esker, our landing strip. The northwesterly gale is roaring directly across it. Out of the corner of my eye I glance at Blair. His face is inscrutable. His right hand is up on the power levers between us on the ceiling of the cockpit. He slowly turns the knobs that control the tension on the levers, and eases the power back. The torque gauges drop from 44 to 25; the engines' din becomes a pleasant, steady hum. The computer is blinking: "Arrival at ESKER NOW."

We pull into a steep bank over the ridgetop. I see people moving out of the tents and peering upward. From 200 feet above them I can read the expressions on their faces: they're surprised to see us. We circle again and turn away to line up an approach. Blair calls for twenty degrees of flaps; I position the flap lever and answer him, "Flaps coming twenty."

"Hit those wipers, will you?"

I fumble for the switch and find it; the wiper blades begin bouncing back and forth across the windshield. We are on final approach, crablike in our descent as Blair compensates for the crosswind. "Gimme full flaps."

"Roger, full flaps."

"Props fine."

"Roger." The propellers set up a high vibrato as they rotate into beta range, ready to generate reverse thrust. The base of the esker rushes up. Six or eight people huddle there with their backs to the driving rain. At the critical instant Blair aborts the landing and overshoots, calls for flaps to ten degrees, and adds full power to climb away from the strip. I look at him again—he is gazing ahead, flying the airplane, expressionless as can be. "Windy!" he says over the intercom.

We line up again. He calls for thirty degrees of flaps this time and asks me to put the wiper blades on high. The little wiper arms dance across the windshield at a frantic pace; we're dropping fast again toward the touchdown spot. Just as we reach it Blair kicks the right rudder pedal hard and drops the left wing low into the wind. The left tire hits ground, followed instantly by the right and the oversized nosewheel. Blair yanks the power levers back and rams the engines into full reverse. We lurch to a halt. Engines whine in opposition as the big plane nimbly pirouettes atop the narrow esker, and we taxi slowly back over the rough ground. I am dumbfounded by the piloting performance I've just watched.

As Blair shuts down the engines I climb over the plywood and propane to reach the cargo door. I swing the door open and there is Vic, the reason for the night's journey. He is beaming. "Wasn't sure you'd make it in this weather."

We make small talk as we unload. The storm has come in quickly; everyone in camp had been wearing shorts earlier in the day. They are setting up for a summer program of drilling and sampling. It feels like it may start to snow.

We throw on a few empty fuel barrels and propane cylinders, fold down a seat for Vic, close the doors, and prepare for takeoff. Blair asks me to hold the control yoke full over to the left until he takes control away from me on the takeoff run. The Twin Otter on wheels or skis is steered with an awkward tiller bar atop the pilot's yoke. For a moment then, here is something truly helpful for me to do. We back up to the edge of the esker and pause at a slight angle into the wind. I check to see that Vic has his seatbelt latched. Blair holds the brakes, puts power to the engines, releases the brakes, and guides the plane for a few yards with the tiller bar. Then I feel the yoke pulled out of my hand and instantly we're in the air, crabbed crosswise to the esker. We turn south toward Yellowknife and begin blistering along with the wind off our tail. Blair turns control over to me for the ride back to the airport. The computer displays the time enroute: 1:46.

At three in the morning we land at Yellowknife. The sky is clear and bright. The streets are deserted. We drop Vic off at his home; he will change clothes and go to the hospital, where his wife has already given birth to their child.

The Twin Otter is a machine that makes routine work of landings on eskertops in rainsqualls, of takeoffs on floats from rough seas, and of setting down on skis amid the jumbled ice blocks at the North Pole. I harbor grave doubts about our petro-fueled civilization, our glittering technology and its effect on the world, but there is a certain thrill that rises within me when I see or hear a bushplane. As the whistle of a freight train rolling through the prairie seems to give voice to humanity's efforts in that landscape, the sound of PT6 turbines spooling up on the tundra is linked in my mind to the rugged vastness of the North.

Last summer I was up on the wing of a Twin Otter on floats, checking the oil at the start of the day. I pulled the dipstick from the top of one engine and wiped it clean. As I tilted it, the clean metal caught the glint of the rising sun. It was five A.M. I thought of a poem by Gary Snyder, called "Why Log Truck Drivers Rise Earlier Than Students of Zen." The final line was, "There is no other life."

I could imagine such an acceptance that morning. I could see how the one life of mine, this airplane flying, could over time usurp and obliterate the other, my life in the bush, my dogs and canoes and log cabins. But it was not obliterating it yet; in many ways it was *strengthening* my ties to the remoteness and distances of the North.

When I saw that glint of light on the turbine-engine dipstick and thought of that poem, I remembered another glint of light, on an evening of deep cold at the end of a cold day—forty below and dropping, the sun long down, firewood still to be gathered. The tent was up, the dogs were waiting to be taken out of harness, but the pressing need was for some heat. I was alone in a small stand of spruce. The moon was just rising. The blade on my bowsaw was new and shiny, and as I tilted it to start my cut, a bright flash of moonlight bounced from the steel. I paused. That glint of moonlight on that saw blade summed up the life I was living at the moment: night, cold, wood, dogs.

Six months later the dipstick gleaming at sunrise meant a day of flying, two or three loads of fuel drums to deliver to a beach on a distant nameless lake. The company for which I was flying was supporting a massive land rush. Diamonds had been discovered on the tundra, and the discovery had set off a frenzy of claim-staking and sampling. The entire area of activity, a square more than 300 miles on a side, was accessible in the summer only by air. Bushplanes hauled stakes, stakers, camp crews, groceries, drillers, geologists, tents, helicopter parts, and turbine fuel out to the barrens. Back to Yellowknife came empty drums, returning workers, broken machinery, and thousands of tons of sand and rock samples in carefully labeled bags. Planes were flying at all hours of the day and night, and the most vital machines in the entire effort were the Twin Otters.

I relished the work. The notion of being a cog in the machinery, of having a task clearly laid out before me and then working to accomplish it, was refreshing. It was a wonderful respite from the self-directed, self-motivated days at the Hoarfrost River—building, writing, training dogs. The pay was good, and every morning as I strapped myself into that worn co-pilot's seat on the right side of the cockpit I was there—*right there* and nowhere else, in a way that has at certain times been hard for me to find.

Still, while flying I found myself wavering and shifting between two levels. I struggled to exist fully in one—*there is no other life*—and always could sense another broader, wondering view. If I was guiding a Twin Otter down the final approach to a lake, a part of me was off to one side, marvelling that this pair of chairs, these two men, these 5,000 pounds of freight and fuel and 8,500 pounds of airplane were all hurtling downward through thin air at a hundred miles an hour. There was the touch of my warm, sweat-dampened hand on the knurled metal power levers, the silk-smooth deceleration of the turbines... *Concentrate! Concentrate!* I would try to do *nothing more* than hold the airspeed at 80 knots and lock the needle of the vertical speed indicator on 500, but still there was that insistent sensation of wonder.

Ten feet above the water then, flaring, air speed bleeding away, I would add a gentle touch of power, and the float keels would sound a staccato chatter on the wave-tops. *Full reverse.* We were down on the lake, taxiing nonchalantly toward shore like a huge ungainly boat, and my heart was pounding wildly, every damned time.

As the summer wore on I settled in. There was no other life. My log-book filled with entries, destinations that until then I had only heard of or read about: Great Bear Lake, Ursus Islands, Contwoyto, Arctic Sound, Cambridge Bay, Coppermine River. "Dropped stakers," "picked up canoeists," "looked for geology crew," "moved police and prisoners," "slept in plane waiting for daylight..." "last flight of season."

By then I was eager to go home to our cabin on the shore, to wood-piles and sled dogs and bowsaw blades gleaming dimly in the moonlight.

WOLVERINE TRACKS

Ten years ago I bought a small wolverine pelt from a trapper in Reliance. That dark brown pelt with its blonde edges, cut carefully into pieces, provided trim for hoods on five different parkas over the years. Those parkas are used hard for seven months of each twelve, and one by one those ruffs have worn out; the guard hairs which gave them their effectiveness are all but gone on two of the hoods. It is time for me to acquire another wolverine pelt, with which to keep our hoods trimmed for another ten or fifteen years.

There is no fur as good as wolverine for trimming a parka hood. In bitter cold one's breath condenses and freezes on the fur trim, and wolverine hair is coarse enough for the frost to be brushed with the flick of a mitten. A fur ruff around the hood of a winter parka is a wonderful advantage. It creates a pocket of calm air around one's face and seals the neck and head from drafts. On a day of forty or fifty below zero and even a slight breeze, such as the flow of air in the wake of a moving dogteam, the difference between a trimmed and an untrimmed hood is great.

My hunt for another wolver-

55

ine pelt—for I am determined not to purchase this one—has been relatively simple, unburdened by confounding questions about the fur trade. The animals are abundant here where I live, I have good use for the entire pelt, and there is no material available anywhere that will provide such effective protection from frostbite. Tender human noses and cheeks are best preserved in their entirety; wolverine fur enables that preservation.

Legally I am entitled to shoot a wolverine, but not to trap one. The tag for the privilege costs me five dollars. The rules are simple: no closed season, no closed area, no limit, no selling of the fur. Five years ago I bought one tag, and every autumn since then I have bought another. Still no wolverine. With the region's trappers shipping a dozen or more wolverine pelts to market each year, my quest is becoming a standing joke around here. My ongoing hunt, though, like all hunts for animals, has brought me closer to this most mysterious and elusive mammal of the far north.

The wolverine, *Gulo luscus*, is a member of the taxonomic family Mustelidae. This family includes weasels, skunks, marten, otters, and badgers. Adult wolverines range in weight from thirty-five to sixty pounds, stand ten to fourteen inches tall, and measure three to four feet from tip of nose to tip of tail. A wolverine looks like a cross between a badger and a bear. Its coat is of thick coarse fur, deep brown or nearly black in midwinter, with a striking blonde stripe that runs back from the shoulders and over the top of the rump. In the steady daylight of arctic spring the entire coat becomes bleached to a straw yellow. The animal's head is small in proportion to its broad, powerful torso.

The wolverine is an opportunist by trade. It roams a large area in search of food, and thrives in places where there seems to be absolutely nothing to eat—the barrenlands in January, for instance. Wolverines often feed on the leftover remains of caribou killed by wolves or people, and they are legendary in the North for their cleverness and audacity in the pilfering of caches, outpost camps, and traplines. The reputation of the wolverine among that small group of trappers who are familiar with the animal has long been one of fierceness, cunning, courage, and tremendous strength.

I first came across the tracks of a wolverine on a cross-country ski trip near Hoodoo Pass in the Rocky Mountains. Just above timberline on a corniced ridge that formed the Idaho-Montana border, I saw what I thought at first were wolf tracks. But there were five toeprints, and a wolf or a dog shows only four. Twenty years later, the print of a fifth toe in a blurred track is still, for me, the surest confirmation that a track was left by a wolverine.

The sight of a wolverine track in Montana was a rare coincidence. Wolverines now thrive only in northern Canada and Alaska, in the most remote stretches of a range that once swept south well into the midwestern and mountain states. Michigan—the Wolverine State—actually was at one time home to wolverines, but it is no longer. Amidst our civilization's ongoing invasion of this continent's wild lands, that odd five-toed track is today a stamp of genuine remoteness.

The day of my first glimpse of a wolverine is still the day I came closest to shooting one. It was a Sunday in mid-November, 1987, and I was on skis travelling east from our cabin on the new ice of McLeod Bay. The bay was frozen to a mile or so offshore; beyond that, wave-tossed open water steamed in the cold. At that season the new ice forms an avenue between land and water—a wide boulevard for the easy movement of caribou, wolves, foxes, and wolverines. I skied along the shore for a few miles into a rising wind, then turned back for home. Almost immediately I saw the unmistakable five-toed footprints of a wolverine in the skiff of snow that covered the ice. The tracks came northeast from the ice edge, joined my ski tracks, shuffled confusedly, and started west. The wolverine was ahead of me, and not by far.

I checked my rifle: four bullets in the magazine. I could almost see that new pelt, those new lengths of parka trim. I hurried west, peering into the afternoon's gray dimness. There was an animal moving there—not a wolverine but Kristen's pet Siberian husky, Kasota, bounding gaily toward me along the trail. She had slipped her collar for the hundredth time and taken up my track. I cursed softly. The wolverine would be long gone.

Tracks told the first part of the story. At what must have been the moment Kasota came into sight, the wolverine had left my ski trail and turned toward the thick forest near the mouth of the Hoarfrost. I slowed to a dejected shuffle, sweating hard, wondering how close I might have come were it not for the loose dog. I half-heartedly scanned the trees along shore, but I was chilly and soon turned for the cabin.

Kristen had watched the entire episode. Just after my departure she had seen a dark animal lope across the ice a hundred yards offshore. It was headed east, and through the binoculars she confirmed that it was a wolverine—the first that either of us had ever seen. She knew I had a rifle along, not the little .22 for ptarmigan, but the 30.06 carbine. Smiling, wondering what might happen, she had gone back inside. The barking of the dogs had alerted her to Kasota's escape, and she had gone out in time to watch her pet dash pell-mell across the ice toward the wolverine's trail and my ski tracks.

Wolverines are unpredictable. While I was inside warming up and making disparaging remarks about Kasota, this one was looping back across the ridges north of the cabin. It emerged onto the ice in front of the homestead for the second time in an hour, again headed east. The barking of the dogs sounded the alarm again, and there was a mad scramble as I put my skis back on, grabbed the rifle, closed the door on Kasota, and pushed off for a second chance.

The ungainly gait of a wolverine was described well by a neighbor of ours: "like a football bouncing down the ice." The gait is not fast, no match for a hunter roaring along on a snowmobile, but it is surprisingly tireless. As I hurried after that wolverine I did not gain on it. I skied as fast as I could and nearly went down in a heap several times when the tip of my ski pole slipped on the hard new ice. I saw that I might have one chance as the wolverine circled behind two rock islands just east of the rivermouth. There was a bay back there; by cutting between the islands I might close the gap a bit.

A wolverine does not second-guess itself. Most animals, when chased, will pause every so often to reevaluate the situation. The wolverine, nine times out of ten, does not break stride. For a marksman like me, no expert at hitting a moving target, the wolverine's unhesitating retreat offers no chance to take steady aim. One must shoot on the fly or not at all.

I reached the gap between the two islands. I was completely winded as I crouched behind a boulder and pumped a shell into the firing chamber of the gun. The wolverine rounded the south end of the offshore island and started across the bay. I fired four times, each bullet sent up a harmless puff of snow above or below or behind the animal, and the gun was empty. I dug into my pocket for more shells, but the distance between us was soon close to two hundred yards. By the time I had reloaded, the wolverine had gained the shore and disappeared over a rise of rock, never looking back and never breaking that bouncing-football lope. I skied home, wishing that I'd brought a camera with a long lens instead of my rifle. A wolverine—the first I'd ever seen.

Two years later I had what might have been a good chance to shoot a wolverine, but this time I hesitated. It was another November day during freeze-up, and both Kristen and I were working outdoors. Suddenly she ran toward me, talking in a soft voice, "I think there's a wolverine on that little island. McLeod sees him."

We had seen a red fox earlier in the day, so I was skeptical; I figured the fox had come back. McLeod and Grayling both had their noses high in the air. They sniffed and stared at a little point southwest of them. In no great hurry I walked to the house, rummaged for some bullets, loaded the gun, and ambled down to the shoreline.

Had I been more careful I might have surprised him, but instead he surprised me. Kristen began shouting, "There it goes—there it is!" and pointing ahead of me. I broke into a run and topped the little island. There it went indeed—a huge dark wolverine charging straight across the bay. I knelt to shoot, but I paused.

That bay had been open water until that very morning, and I'd been over there a few hours earlier to test the ice with a hatchet. It was about an inch thick. Not even a wolverine pelt was going to get me out on that ice until at least the next day. By then the ravens would have torn into the carcass and ruined the fur. I watched the wolverine go, fully expecting him to break through as he reached the center of the bay. On he went. I slung the gun over my shoulder and watched him reach the far shore, safe and sound. That was twice.

A third chance came the following spring in almost the same place. Friends of ours from Yellowknife, Peter and Teri and their two young sons, had paid us a surprise visit one Saturday morning. It was early May, the first warm day of the spring thaw. The plane they flew was a Cessna 185 on skis, and with it parked on the lake ice just offshore we had settled down to visit at the table in front of the house.

Kristen spotted something out on the bay, just a tiny dark dot about a mile to the southwest. She brought out the binoculars and confirmed her guess—it was a wolverine. There was a caribou carcass on the ice out there, where the wolves had brought a yearling down a few days earlier. I knew because I'd passed by it on a dogsled only hours after the kill. Now the wolverine was at the spot, cleaning up whatever the wolves had left.

"You get a wolverine *yet?*" Peter asked with a grin.

"Nope."

"Well get your rifle."

We climbed into the plane. A hasty runup, full power, and we were airborne, eighty feet above the ice heading straight for the wolverine at a hundred miles an hour. Almost immediately Peter was chopping the power, yanking down the wingflaps, and flaring to land. The wolverine had abandoned the caribou carcass and was making for shore at a dead

run. We touched down alongside the scattered chunks of bone and pieces ·
of caribou skin, and slid, and slid, and slid over the ice. "Damned thing
takes forever to stop on skis," Peter shouted. I was fumbling with the rifle,
my seatbelt, and the door handle all at once.

At last the plane stopped and I jumped out. The wolverine was on
top of the shoreline cliff, broadside to us at perhaps 130 yards. He was
on the run, without a pause or a backward glance. I knelt and fired. He
seemed to break stride almost imperceptibly; for a moment I expected him
to crumple and fall. On he went. I fired once more, and we heard the bullet ricochet from the sloping rock wall.

We wallowed without snowshoes up the steep slope through soggy,
waist-deep drifts. There in the wolverine's track was a single dot of blood,
not more than twice the size of this printed O—one drop. So maybe he
had skipped a beat, as we both thought we'd seen. But there was no more
blood anywhere to be found. After slogging alongside the track for a quarter mile, Peter and I were convinced that the wolverine was long gone and
in good health. We went back to the plane for the short hop home.

After that brief hunt there was a drought in my wolverine sightings
that stretched on for nearly two years. I wondered if I had cursed my luck
by resorting to an airplane. Tracks of wolverines were abundant all
through the hills north of our homestead, and our trails that next winter
were absolutely crisscrossed with wolverine sign. Meanwhile, our parka
ruffs were steadily wearing thin, encouraging my ongoing hunt. On countless training runs with the dogs, logging thousands of miles between
October and April, I packed the rifle in a handy spot on top of the sled
load. Again and again I crossed a fresh trail, convinced more than once
that a wolverine was watching me from the shoreline trees, but still I saw
nothing.

On a spring dogteam trip with three other mushers the jinx finally
ended. On a cold April evening we had camped just northwest of Artillery
Lake. We were two days into a five-day trip, on a big loop north and east
of our homestead.

By late April the daylight stretches well into the night and there is no
urgency to the work of making camp. With the fire blazing to melt snow
for water, the tent up, and our supper started, I was free to have a look
around. I walked toward the edge of the little grove of spruce and tamarack. Out there on the lake ice, at long last, was a wolverine. It was broadside to me, loping slowly along, pausing, turning, and sniffing, making its
evening rounds.

Arleigh was putting some salve on one of his dogs' feet. Chris was cooking dinner. Jim was walking up the ridge east of camp. I was already wearing my snowshoes, and my rifle was slung from the handlebar of my sled. I pointed to the wolverine, by then nearly out of sight over a small rise, and announced to Arleigh and Chris that I was going to follow it on foot.

I had a good feeling about that one. I swung along on the hard crust of the lake. The wolverine was out of sight; I could make good time gaining on it. I had two clips of four shells each, shells which I had loaded specifically for this purpose. They were 150-grain bullets, lighter than the standard, with full metal jackets and a reduced load of gunpowder in the cartridge. They would make a neat round hole in a wolverine pelt, instead of a jagged blast that would ruin more of the precious fur. The odds seemed good that after nearly six years this would be my night.

A line of tracks crossed directly in front of me, and I stopped short. The tracks had five toeprints, and there was a long, deep claw mark about an inch ahead of each toe. Behind the toes was the clear impression of a large footpad, six inches long and three or four inches wide. The tracks were fresh, not windblown or melted out: a barren-ground grizzly bear, up and around on April 24 after a season in its den.

Bears hibernate, more or less, in winter; this one had probably been aroused by the warm weather of the past week. The spring had turned suddenly cold again, though, and the temperature that night was far below zero. The snow cover on the lakes and tundra formed a hard crust lightly dusted with a skiff of fresh powder. Thoroughly surprised, but still intent on my chase, I moved forward. A few more strides brought me to the fresh trail of the wolverine.

It was fascinating to follow those wolverine tracks that evening, because the animal did not know it was being pursued. Instead of making a beeline for the nearest escape, the trail crossed the tundra in a zigzag of investigation. The tracks showed frequent pauses and turns where the wolverine had scratched up an old caribou antler, sniffed some ptarmigan droppings, hopped up onto a boulder and back down again, and just browsed and perused the countryside on the lookout for a meal.

I had put the grizzly tracks out of my thoughts. I could tell the others about them, and they could come have a look. I was excited by the prospect of gaining ground on this wolverine; I figured I was moving at least twice as fast as it was. The tracks wandered down to another arm of the lake. I strained to spot any movement along the foot of a big sand esker that rose from the far shore. If the wolverine had gone that way, the game was over—the esker system was a maze of thickets, little pothole lakes, and steep bluffs.

My luck held. At the shoreline the tracks turned toward a patch of small spruce trees at the head of a cove. I paused and advanced a shell into the firing chamber. If there was anything of interest to it in that thicket, and surely there would be *something* in there, that was where the wolverine would be. I stood still and searched carefully with my eyes, scrutinizing the thicket piece by piece.

There was a big round rock in there, an oddly shaped boulder strangely free of snow, with a gradual taper to it. It was partly hidden behind some trees. At the top of it two rounded nubs looked almost like ears. I held my breath, slowly realizing. The boulder stood up.

My heart was pounding. I'd seen grizzly bears before, but I'd never met one except when I was seated safely in a canoe, the bear on shore at some comfortable distance. Now I was on solid wind-packed snow, staring at a bear that was staring right back at me, with about fifty yards between us. Its tracks had looked big to me, and the grizzly itself looked gigantic. Barren-ground grizzlies in the Northwest Territories are not big grizzlies. I knew that even a full-grown male rarely weighed more than 400 pounds, but still this bear stood every inch of six feet tall. He was sniffing the air. It looked as if he was trying to determine just what I was.

The standard words of wisdom about bear encounters were fresh in my mind. A week earlier I'd been out on the trail with a group of doctors who were conducting a field seminar. One of the topics they had discussed had been bear attacks and bear behavior.

"The worst thing you can do is run. On level ground a grizzly might hit thirty miles an hour. You won't outrun it and by running you'll entice it to chase you."

I thought about my rifle and those measly little metal-jacket bullets with which it was loaded. Those were not the bullets with which to stop a grizzly's charge, except perhaps at the moment when the gun barrel could be placed inside the bear's mouth. I took one cautious step backward on my snowshoes. The bear immediately dropped to all fours and moved decisively toward me with three or four powerful, supple steps. I made another move back. He, or she, came forward out of the trees and onto the lake, stopped, sniffed, and sat down on his haunches again. I could clearly see the dish-shaped face and the hump above the shoulders. There was a breath of breeze flowing from the bear back toward me; I almost thought I could smell it. We each held our distance for several long minutes, as I slowly eased back up the gradual slope of the low rise that separated me from our camp. The bear moved ahead, paused, moved ahead, and paused. The gap between us gradually widened to a hundred yards or more, but the bear stayed right on my trail and kept its gaze fixed on me.

I thought about speaking to the bear; Chris had told me that he had done this in the Brooks Range, where he led trips during the summer. He said he thought it let the bear know what a person was—he just talked loudly and told the bear he hadn't intended to surprise it, and usually it moved away. But I stayed quiet and kept backing up. Finally I came to the top of the rise. When the ridge cut off the bear's view of me, I turned toward camp and broke into a run.

One of my snowshoes caught a ridge of snow crust and immediately fell off. I paused long enough to pick it up, but not long enough to put it back on. I dashed along with a snowshoe in one hand and my rifle in the other, debating as I went as to which of my feet was making better time. Then over my shoulder I saw the bear again, silhouetted on the skyline of the ridge. I stopped, breathing hard and perspiring. We were nearly 300 yards apart. The bear started downhill along my trail, then swung back up to the top of the rise and moved north along the crest. Probably it had picked out a whiff of campfire smoke. At last it dropped out of sight on the far side of the hill, back toward where I had first seen it.

I walked back to camp. Just before I got to the dogs and my partners, I thought of the wolverine. My friends were oblivious to what had just happened, and when they saw me they would be watching to see if I was carrying anything.

I grinned as I imagined that wolverine back in that small stand of trees; he had watched me walk straight into that grizzly.

There will be other wolverines. The other day Kristen and I saw one on the tundra near Cook Lake. It was mid-June and the wolverine was sun-bleached completely blonde. It gamboled back and forth, shuffling and sniffing, looping and hurrying in its endless search for something edible. Hidden on a rocky hilltop, we waited while it moved steadily up the slope toward us.

I had left the rifle at home, miles away, and so for once I just watched a wolverine and savoured the pleasure of living in a neighborhood still home to such a vivid embodiment of tenacity, wildness, and mystery.

PREMONITION

In mid-August the geese flew off the tundra, calling excitedly as they passed above the homestead. I noted their migration in my daily record and wondered what it meant. "Could be an early winter" was the consensus of the local sages. We all nodded agreement and watched the wavering Vs go south.

Then the caribou moved, decisively and extravagantly—one could almost say purposefully. They marched south early—and farther to the south than they had come in late summer for many years. We saw a few of them, and the tracks of hundreds more, on a beach just a few miles down the shore of the big lake. That was September 3. "Could be a real early winter," we all pronounced again, and nodded.

Today as I lie under thick quilts in the loft of the cabin, I hear an odd sound. Every morning I lie here just after waking and listen carefully, deciphering the sound of the wind in the trees or the waves on the beach. This morning the lake is making a sound I have not heard for eleven months. The rhythmic roll of the waves is muffled; a swishing, shifting sound infiltrates the thick log walls from all directions, a white noise in the darkness. I roll over to look outside, but this morning a layer of ice covers the pane of the window. With my fingernail I scratch a tiny peephole in the frost, and through it I can just make out the dim line of the beach, the dark expanse of the lake, and between the two a vague pale stripe that is new.

It is slush ice, pans of it in the shallows, carried in by the prevailing easterly wind. The lake has at last succumbed to the constant cold of the past ten days. Early, weeks early.

I climb down the ladder and dress hurriedly in the dark. I shut the door behind me and walk down to the shore. The day's dawn twilight dimly illumines the pier, the boat, the yellow floatplane pulled up on its pole ramp... all bordered by a gently heaving field of loose white ice. The jostling, grating pans extend out into the lake a good thirty or forty feet. A brisk wind pushes them ashore and raises choppy whitecapped waves in the open water beyond.

I think of all that will need to happen here in the coming day or two. We must free the plane from the ice, turn it around, winch it ashore and lift it clear of the ground, take off the floats and bolt on the landing gear wheels. We will have to run the outboard motor dry of gasoline, lift it off the transom, then haul the boat up and roll it over on the beach. It will sit there, buried under drifts of snow blown in from the bay, for eight months. There is still a fishnet in the water up at our outpost camp. So far it will be free of ice, there in the current of a channel, but we will have to lift it soon or risk having it torn apart by the ice.

There is nothing unusual about these annual chores of freeze-up. But as I walk back to the cabin I am startled when I remember the day's date. It is October 8. This swishing ice, this biting wind in my face and the firm frozen beach underfoot, the dusting of snow lying in the hollows—it is all two or three weeks early.

How did they know, those geese flying south three weeks ahead of their accustomed time, those herds of caribou sweeping in from the barrens a full month before we expected them? What messages do they read, what signs do they see or hear or feel from the earth and sky, that they knew so plainly in advance what was coming?

I step inside and stoke the fire, put on the coffeepot, light the lamp, and turn on the radio. I check the thermometer that hangs on the north wall of the old cabin: eleven below zero and still dropping, winter by any standards. And early, just as every other creature here told us it would be.

PHOTOGRAPHS

*Hoarfrost homestead dusted with the first snow of
early October.*

*Migrating caribou swim the Hoarfrost, two miles
above the homestead.*

Change-over from wheels to floats on the
1946 J-3 Cub; June 2.

Taltheili Narrows, at west end of McLeod Bay.

Pan ice along shore, late October.

Jiminy and McDougal lead a team along the upper Hoarfrost on a mid-April trip with a group of visitors.

Dogs take a rest from trail-breaking in soft spring snow.

Crossing a pressure ridge, late May on Great Slave Lake. Two sleds are towed for two people, to ensure better control.

Lacy Falls, late summer.

Migrating caribou ford the river below Lacy Falls.

Four bull caribou in the meadow below Lacy Falls.

Dinner at an April campsite on the Kahochella Peninsula.

Lacy Falls, late winter.

Kristen in the library alcove of the main cabin, with McLeod,
a six-year-old husky.

Our main cabin along the Hoarfrost.

Dave with pups at Obelisk Lake, October.

ESKER

By the spring of 1988, my first here, I had come to know the life and the country just enough to let me feel a bit proud. Things were working out; I had made good progress in less than a year at the homestead. I had made friends with my neighbors, and had nearly succumbed to their hard-edged view of their hermitic world. The region had started to feel like a distant fief, far removed from the world "outside." Here a man was king and court, hunter and gatherer, alone to form his own incontrovertible ideas on things, however slanted and solipsistic.

I felt tough, as if nothing could stop me. The work of the place—hauling and peeling logs, hoisting buckets of water, scraping hides, rolling 400-pound gas drums up the beach—all added to the feeling of *hubris*, of being capable of almost anything, and well within one's rights. Add to that tough feeling a session of gossip and stories, on a long May evening with a few shots of rye whisky, and proud schemes were born, the hopelessness of which would only become clear two or three years later.

We were talking about dogs and wolves that evening. My neighbor, whom I'll call M. here (that is not his initial), is a hunter and trapper and has been for twenty years. He is among the most efficient of modern trappers in the far north—a fearless, straight-shooting master of barren-land and bush. He and his family don't own sled dogs anymore, only a couple of mixed-breed pets small enough to stow in a canvas mailbag for trips by skidoo, big enough for children to play with, and feisty enough to bark at bears. But they had huskies once, old-style "gidde" freight dogs—rangy, tough, and smart. "May be some wolf blood in them not too far back," M. thought. "Lots of the old trappers used to run half or quarter wolves."

I'd been out as a spectator on one of M.'s hunts that first winter, and I'd seen the power and speed of a big Arctic wolf as it fled from us. Kristen and I had an old skidoo on loan from M. that season. With my frostbitten thumb clamping the throttle lever right to the handlebar and the wooden snowdrifts on the bay rattling every bone in my torso, I'd watched a wolf gradually widen the distance between us.

As a wolf hunter or a trapper I was a fake and I knew it, even in those first proud months. My heart was not in the chase. Had I closed the gap on that wolf and decided to take a shot, I would surely have missed. But the wolf so easily outran that old snowmobile, doing an honest thirty miles an hour, that I—a dog musher—was thoroughly impressed.

We poured another inch of whiskey into the glasses, and wondered aloud whether we could find a wolf den and steal a pup or two, sometime in the next week, while they were still young. Breed them down, get to one-quarter or one-eighth wolf over the next few years, and end up with a hybrid that was fast and tough and intelligent, with long legs and a fluid trot and incredibly tough feet. Move back to the origins of dog mushing, against all wise judgement, and start a new breed, right out here in the fief. Yes, yes, it would be interesting. When I visited M. and his family again later that week, to watch the last game of the Stanley Cup finals (successful modern trappers have satellite television), we agreed to go looking for a wolf den on the next clear calm day.

June 5 was a perfect day. There is a season in the far north that is little known outside. It is one of the perks of permanent residence, like the warm, clear week that sometimes comes in early October. In late May and early June the lakes are still solidly frozen, effectively stymying the canoeists and fishermen, and the snow has melted from the land. The ice on the lakes is bounded by a wide, inconvenient moat, a "shore lead" of open water; the creeks and fast sections of rivers are open and running high. Wheels replace skis on the landing gear of airplanes, for landing and taking off on the smooth white surface of the lakes. No mosquitoes or blackflies have hatched, and the sunlight is continuous.

That Saturday I landed our J-3 Cub on wheels at the back end of the bay near M.'s house. He was waiting on the ice with a little pile of gear—dried food, a tin cup, and a jacket. "Got a rifle?" he asked above the noise of the engine.

I nodded. "Rifle, radio, and all that."—the northern flight insurance policy. He climbed in. I thought for a minute about leaving the door down, which when flying low in the Cub gives an exhilarating impression of magical flight, skimming the hilltops in a little winged chair. But it was cool, and it would be cooler up north, so I closed the door and we took off.

We climbed and banked away from M.'s lake, heading toward the steep bluffs that separate the lake basin from the tundra. I had an intercom rigged up that day, so M. and I could easily converse as we flew.

"Where we going?" I asked.

"Oh I dunno. Let's head up the west side of S_____ and check those eskers west from there."

S_____ Lake is almost as big as McLeod Bay—a huge white swath that day, stretching fifty miles ahead of us and eight miles wide in places. It forms a sharp boundary between treeless country and the edge of the spruce forest. We followed the treeless north shore, chugging along at sixty miles an hour a few hundred feet above the brown and gray and light green mosaic of tundra grass, rock, and lichen.

"Nice day," crackled through my headset.

"Yep. Beautiful."

"We should check out those eskers between R_____ and D_____ Lakes; they might have a den on them." I banked northeast. We dropped lower, still flying slow, droning along over meltpools speckled with snowgeese and Canadas, resting there while their nesting grounds to the north thawed. I glanced at my map and found R_____ Lake. I had passed this way twice, years before by dogteam, but it may as well have been new country to me.

R_____ Lake is five or ten miles long and a few miles wide. From its northeast end a series of low esker ridges snake along the tundra toward D_____ Lake. Eskers are the raised beds of meltwater rivers that once flowed beneath the glaciers; they look like winding river channels in bas relief. They are landmarks, passageways, and stopping places in the barrens, often supporting a few straggly stands of spruce trees in protected pockets well past treeline. They are natural walkways for animals and people. In winter their tops are often blown clean of snow, and they stand out like brown roads in the undulating white barrens.

For wolves the eskers provide good den sites, raised above the surrounding country and covered with a thick mat of low vegetation. The roots of the plants bind the sand and gravel, and keep the roof of the den safe from collapse. I imagine too that a nursing female wolf appreciates the breeze and sunshine of an esker top, as she lies with her pups once they have grown big enough to emerge from the den.

We had flown a few miles along a prominent esker when M. spotted a wolf running away from the sound of the plane. We passed over her and circled; she threw frightened glances upward at us as she fled. Wolves in this country have survived by being scared, and fast, and absolutely cautious in any situation involving humans. We thought we had scared this wolf *away* from something, but she was not likely to lead us *toward* any place important to her. I say "she" because to me she looked like a female. I thought I could even detect an odd heaviness in her abdomen—a wobble as she ran, that might have been the weight of milk-filled mammaries.

We circled back over the spot where M. had first seen her, and back along a braided series of esker ridges. We could see no sign of a den, but we agreed that this place would be worth a closer look. I brought the plane around and the tires gently bumped the smooth white ice of D_____ Lake, in a narrow bay just south of the esker. I let the engine run and cool at idle for a few minutes, then switched it off. A wonderful silence followed the last puff of combustion.

We stepped out onto the ice. With the firm white expanse of the lake underfoot and the engine quiet, the beauty of the day was palpable again. Flying is a marvelous means of scouting new country, of transporting freight and people, and of changing one's perspective on the world, but I am always left a bit stunned by the speed and roar of it. It is always good to get out of the plane, tie it down, and walk away from it into whatever new place it has landed.

I put some lunch and a little gas stove into my knapsack, along with a canvas bag to hold whatever we might find. We started up the south slope of the esker through deep drifts of melting snow. At the top we split up, each following some notion of where a den might be, following faint leads but mostly just enjoying a walk in the barrens on a June day.

90

I picked up a line of fresh wolf tracks along the northeast slope of the northernmost ridge. A worn walkway dipped and wove just below the crest, showing movement in both directions, and I traced it northeast. A shout from M. was carried on the light breeze, and I turned to see him a quarter-mile back, waving and smiling. I trotted toward him, smiling myself.

The top of the esker there was laced tightly with roots of gnarled, wind-blasted spruce and a thick mat of low-bush cranberry plants. Tracks, bits of whitened bone, and tufts of fur were scattered on the sloping sand shelf before a round, dark hole. "I'll be damned," I said.

M. suddenly canted his head. He is slowly going deaf from too many gunshots and too much engine noise, but still he had heard something. I heard it then myself—a plaintive chorus of tiny whimpers rising from deep in the hillside. Pups.

I'd heard that thready whimper a hundred times, from the whelping pens back at the dog yard. It is a sound of spring for me, like the song of the first robin. There *were* pups in there; that *had* been their mother running away from us.

M. puffed softly on a cigarette. "Too bad we don't have a shovel," he said, ever one for the direct approach. I nodded, but I wasn't listening to him. In my imagination I was down in that hole, finding out that in fact the mother *hadn't* run away over the hill—that had been some other member of the pack. Crammed downward in the sloping tunnel, what was I going to do when a mother wolf met me face to face?

I told myself she couldn't be in there. If she was, why were the pups whimpering like that, in precisely the same tones that I'd heard when nursing bitches stepped out of their houses to eat or drink, leaving their pups unattended? Hadn't I read that the mother would try to lure us away, confident that we wouldn't find the den on our own?

This wolf-pup stealing has a long and checkered history. I'd read the accounts of Olaus Murie, who worked in McKinley National Park in Alaska in the 1940s. He and his wife had raised pups that they'd stolen from a den. So had some of the modern wolf biologists whose names I recognized; they had raised orphans or homeless captives in order to study their development.

The barrenland eskers north of Great Slave Lake have a dubious tradition of wolf-pup theft, too. As recently as the 1960s there was a bounty on every pair of wolf ears turned in to the government wildlife department. M. had told me about one no-nonsense Chipewyan trapper who, in those years of the bounty, would walk the eskers in the spring, dig up pups, kill them with a knock on the head, and cut off their ears. It was a source of extra cash for him and many others, money that could buy another case of canned milk, perhaps, for his own growing family. Grim business, but distant and hard to imagine until I found myself on the side of the esker, with the mother wolf scared away and the pups crying.

I scuffed the sand with the toe of my boot, looking down, thinking for the first time about the actual doing of what we had set out that morning to do. M. stood there smoking, looking around, his feet spread wide. Up until that moment we'd been two buddies out on a lark, happy for an excuse to chase around the tundra in the airplane. I for one had not believed that we would actually find a den.

"I guess I'll go in there and see what's up," I announced.

M. evidently hadn't considered that approach. He stiffened suddenly and said, "Down there? You mean crawl down the tunnel?" (Now I was getting my nerve up; this was going to work. *Especially* if M. figured it would be a bit of a risk.)

"Came here to get wolf pups, didn't we? Well, there they are. We may as well have a look at them."

I knelt at the mouth of the tunnel and pursed my lips, sucking in air to make a tight squeaking noise. Depending upon the age of the pups— they sounded much smaller than we'd expected them to be—perhaps they would come out to see what the noise was, like my husky pups did at home.

I squeaked and squeaked, and stuck my head into the mouth of the tunnel. I paused and heard them whimpering again. They sounded tiny, as if perhaps they'd been born within the past week, and they sounded as though they were a long way down into the side of the esker. I squirmed a few feet farther into the opening. My eyes began to adjust to the darkness; the sand on my palms was cold. The tunnel was narrow, about twenty inches in diameter, and it sloped downhill. More whimpering; it was at least ten feet down to the den. I backed out.

I shook the sand out of my hair. "I guess I'll go down there."

"What if there's a wolf in there?"

"Oh, I'm pretty sure the only wolves in there are about the size of a pound of butter."

M. held out his big skinning knife. "At least take this down there with you. You can dig with it, if nothing else."

There was a real danger in going down into the den, but it was not from a wolf, and certainly not from the pups. If the tunnel collapsed, tons of half-frozen sand would fall down on top of me. I walked up onto the top side of the esker and examined the weaving of the tree roots above the tunnel and den, the thick growth of the cranberry plants. It looked very secure. Still, I took M.'s knife from him; it would be good to have something to dig with.

I crouched at the mouth of the tunnel again, with a cigarette lighter in one hand—we'd forgotten to bring a flashlight—and that hefty knife in the other. "Well, Marlin, I'm going in," I joked. "Wild Kingdom" must not have been a part of M.'s childhood television fare, for he gave me a blank look.

It was a journey down and back into an ancient winter, with that clean cold esker sand pressing all around me. Six feet in, with only the soles of my boots still out in daylight, I could feel the steep angle of the downslope as the blood rushed to my head. M. had a grip on my ankles, and his strong hands were reassuring. I lit the lighter. Glistening ice crystals sparkled from the sand wall two inches from my temple. Arms outstretched, lighter and knife out in front, I wormed my way downward and arrived at a bend in the tunnel, a tight turn to the left with a small alcove off on the right side. I thought for a minute it might be a turn-out area in case two wolves met head-on down there, but it didn't seem big enough to serve for that.

"How are you doing in there?" M.'s voice came down. "I'm halfway in myself now."

"It's O.K., I'm fine. No problem."

"You almost down to them?"

"Yeah, I think so. I think I'm close."

The tunnel narrowed, and I could feel fifteen tons of cold sand pressing down on me. A wave of fear crested and subsided again. I backed up and chopped at the sand with the knife. It fell from the walls and roof in jagged lumps. The tunnel was tall enough, but not very wide. "Pupupupup," I called in falsetto.

"What's that?"

"Just talkin' to my puppies; it's O.K."

I squirmed ahead, gained a few more feet, and flicked the little lighter again. A foot and a half ahead of me the passage widened. I inched forward, pushing with the tips of my toes and pulling with my elbows, arms outstretched.

Aha! A tiny peephole of daylight shone brightly from high on the far side of a wide space. I could see a dome-shaped oval room, about four-teen inches high and three-and-a-half feet across. In the center, piled and squirming atop each other, were four, tiny dark pups.

I tried to pull my camera from my coat pocket, but I could not get my arms down past my shoulders. I tried to relax and look carefully, tried to memorize every minute detail of the moment.

"I'm pretty well down in here myself now," said M. from up the tun-nel, still with a firm grip on my ankles. He is over six feet tall, as am I, so altogether I was about thirteen feet into the esker. The little glint of day-light on the far side of the den suddenly looked very inviting. I reached forward and gathered in the pups, holding them as well as I could in the half-crook of my elbows, the knife and lighter still in my hands.

"O.K. I've got 'em! If you can pull me, go ahead and pull!"

M.'s vise grip tightened, and I was drawn back up the passageway in one great heave. In a few seconds we were out, blinking in the sunlight, laughing and shaking sand from our clothes and hair, with the four pups piled at my feet.

They were a bit bigger than they had sounded from far down the tun-nel, but they were not very old. Their eyes were still closed. (They would not open their eyes for another four days, which put their age at nine or ten days on the day we entered the den.) They weighed about two pounds apiece. They were dark, almost pure black, stubby and round, with little pleated wrinkles and lines of lighter fur on their tiny muzzles. Three were males and one, very slightly smaller, was female.

I had hoped to take two females. I thought that the females would be smaller when full-grown—and thus less costly to feed and that they might be less aggressive than males. All of this was conjecture, and it was clear that if I wanted two wolves I would have to take one of each sex. I tipped each of the males upside down in my hand, one at a time. The first two squirmed and whined, desperately trying to roll upright, flailing their stubby legs. The third, a slightly smaller pup, just lay still. I set him aside along with the female.

With the two larger and more rambunctious males in my hands, I inched back down the tunnel on the knobs of my elbows. At first I was determined to return the two pups clear back to the den room, but my gumption failed. Back within the dark and cold of the esker, the cold weight pressing down on my back again, I suddenly felt as though I was pushing my luck. Six feet down in the tunnel I left the little fellows piled together. I was certain that they would be all right until Mom returned; I had seen tiny husky pups survive alone for hours at much lower temperatures.

I came out blinking into the sunlight again. "Let's get out of here," I said, not intending to sound so much like a fleeing criminal. I loaded the two pups into a heavy Canada Post mailbag, and put that into my knapsack. I left the top end of the bag and the pack open for ventilation. M. stamped out his smoke and turned up the hill. For some reason I leaned over and picked up the cigarette butt, and put it in my pocket. I paused briefly to see if I could find the little window of daylight I'd seen from down in the den room; it must have been right there in the side of the esker. I looked back at the tunnel opening, and tried to envision the length and curve and slope of the passageway.

My stomach was fluttering. I felt as if I had crossed some barricade, or dashed into some official place where I didn't belong. I couldn't locate the peephole in the hillside. I topped the esker and headed back toward the plane, suppressing the urge to break into a trot.

My imagination was churning out images. I could see those two already, romping with the dogs at home as they grew up, fathering and mothering litters of tough, intelligent, active pups—pups with a unique gait, a fluidity of movement, and a wild, gently proud spirit. This was going to be something.

We loafed for a while over a pot of tea on the far side of the esker, examined fresh grizzly scat full of the previous autumn's berries, and found some caribou and muskox sign along the crest of the ridge above the airplane. I stopped at least three times to check the two little wolves in the packsack. Two hours after we arrived, the propeller wound up again, the tires bounced from the ice, and I turned the plane back across the esker to pass over the site of the den.

We had been away from there for nearly an hour by then. There was no sign of change. Perhaps the mother wolf had already returned and gone down into the den. Perhaps she was still afraid to return. Perhaps a grizzly would happen past, hear those little cries, and dig up the hillside for a couple of rich morsels. I circled and stared, hoping, but no adult wolf stood calmly at the entrance to the den. I turned south, climbing through 2,000 feet.

We made a day of it, landing at M.'s little camp on the shore of another lake to pick up a window he'd wanted to use elsewhere. We cruised from there to the headwaters of the Hoarfrost, and landed at another old camp M. and his wife had used years earlier. There we salvaged an old kerosene heater. With window, heater, and wolf pups all piled in the tiny baggage compartment behind M., I felt as though we had been out on a Saturday tour of Arctic flea markets. We were getting low on gas when we finally came back within sight of M.'s lake.

The ice had melted steadily in the hours we'd been away. I landed where I had in the morning, and we made our way to shore in a small row-boat. I showed the pups to M.'s family, paddled back out to the plane, and took off alone on the twenty-minute flight to our homestead.

I had a mother husky, Rajah, who was nursing five three-week-old pups in a big whelping pen. I had a plan to follow, the same tactic I'd used to get orphaned puppies accepted by surrogate mothers. Rajah, herself a wolfish-looking dog from the villages of the lower Yukon River, would be the wet nurse for the two little wolves. The two-week gap in the ages of the two litters was obvious. The husky pups' eyes were open, and they were much more alert and lively than the two dark blind newcomers.

Rajah was a conscientious mother, always concerned when she was separated from her pups. In the hour that I kept her apart from the box of puppies, she whined and howled and pawed at the fence of her pen. I tried to ignore her as I tied down the plane, made my dinner, and fed the rest of the dogs.

The idea was to give all seven pups a similar scent, and thus to fool Rajah into accepting and caring for them all as her own. When I brought the enlarged litter back to Rajah that evening, it was obvious that she was not deceived. She welcomed her own pups back, and they burrowed imme-diately into her milk-filled belly. I watched apprehensively as she sniffed Cub and Esker, rolled them over, and began to lick them. Within a minute she nudged them in amongst her own pups, licked them some more, and contentedly sprawled as all the pups nursed. With Cub and Esker sucking eagerly on Rajah's teats, I turned toward the cabin in the cool light of the June midnight. The transplant appeared to be successful.

The wolf pups grew steadily, and in perfect health. I weighed them every two days, and they gained weight in increments of several ounces. By June 7 Cub had one eye open; Esker's eyes were still closed. Two days later all eyes were wide open, and in my notes for that day I wrote that both pups were "very vocal, low steady hum and some whining."

I was living alone that June. The homestead was in its first full round of summer progress, and I was busy. The notes I kept on Cub and Esker are terse and sporadic. On June 14 they were left alone with Rajah; the husky pups were weaned by then. Three days later Esker weighed 4-1/2 pounds and Cub a quarter pound more. "Both will growl if surprised." That night I separated them from Rajah, in order to build up their appetites for an introduction to solid food. In the morning Esker ate a little of the gruel I offered, but Cub ate none, and they were both happy when Rajah returned to feed them herself.

After 5 1/2 years I must refer to my notes to fill in the details of those weeks. I recall the two pups becoming more and more bold as they tottered around the 8 x 8 foot whelping pen. I tried to make time to spend with them each day, and to get them accustomed to being picked up, petted, and spoken to. I was naively optimistic that they could be raised as dogs and that thus they would become dogs in almost every way. On June 20 they were "calm and happy to be picked up, turned over, and patted." A week later they were lapping at a mixture of warm water, ground moose meat, and commercial dog-food. I put the husky pups into the pen with them that night, and cryptically recorded "much interaction." I remember feeling proud. This was going to be easier than I thought.

On June 29, when the pups were about thirty-three days old, a group of canoeists from Minnesota camped near here. That was a thought-provoking day for me, the first of many such days with the captive wolves. In northern Minnesota over 2,000 wolves still range, forming the only viable population of wild wolves in the lower forty-eight states. Along with the loon the wolf has become a potent symbol and figurehead, a totem animal, among those who cherish the Boundary Waters country. That day I fielded the first of many skeptical questions as to the purpose and propriety of stealing and raising wolf pups. I sheepishly learned that I was not immune to the self-aggrandizement that has always seemed to me to lurk within the motives of people who keep captive wolves and wolf-dog hybrids.

I led the group on. Without any explanation I took the pups—five huskies and two wolves—out of the pen and stood back, smiling, while everyone fawned over them. I had seen this many times, with litter after litter of plump, adorable puppies. Then someone asked me about the differences in size, and the two darker, smaller pups with "the different look about them."

I replied casually, "Those two are kind of special."

"Are they from a different mother?"

"They sure are; their mother isn't here."

Tense silence.

"They're wolf pups. Their mother is a wolf."

Expecting to glimpse interest, maybe even admiration in the eyes of the woman holding Esker, I saw instead a flash of confusion and a sudden awkwardness. The group shuffled a bit, and Bill spoke up.

"Why do you have them?" His tone was not indicting, but it certainly did not hold the curiosity and enthusiasm I'd grown used to by then with my neighbors and friends.

I rushed ahead. "I'm raising them as dogs. For breeding. I'll breed them in with the dogs and try to get some of the physical traits they have. They were raised on a dog; they eat dog food. A lot of the old timers used to do this, you know, breed in wolves with their teams, and it worked out O.K."

Everyone smiled and nodded, but the gestures were slow and polite. I could feel the barrier that had fallen between us, but my confidence remained unshaken. I had considered my motives and my methods, and to me, in the outback, they still seemed acceptable. I told myself that the reaction of the visitors was only an indication of some of the changes that had taken place within me since I had moved north.

That night, while I was down at the group's campsite eating dinner with them, enjoying talk of old haunts in the Boundary Waters and Quetico Park, Cub disappeared.

At that time Cub and Esker weighed only 6 1/2 pounds, but although they could not run fast they could cover distance and hold a straight course. Apparently that is what Cub did that evening, toddling straight out of his familiar territory. When I got home and found him gone, I searched the surrounding area for over an hour in thick clouds of mosquitoes. The next morning, before the visitors paddled away, I enlisted their help, and we swept the woods and rock outcrops around the dog yard, pausing and listening and moving back and forth in a systematic search. Nothing.

For the next three days a cold wind brought rain from the northeast. I continued to search half-heartedly for Cub, but I did not hold out much hope. The first few months of any puppy's life hold a long gauntlet of dangers: parvovirus and its relatives, slip-ups around water or ice, the intentional or accidental aggression of older dogs, and the prospect of simply getting lost. There was no shortage of possibilities for Cub's demise, but I found no clues. I gave him up for lost, and turned my attention completely to Esker. The group from Minnesota flew away at the end of their trip, and the doubts they had raised retreated to the back of my mind.

Cub's disappearance was a mystery, but not a huge disappointment. I had been somewhat concerned by the fact that I had two wolf pups. I had guessed that Cub, particularly, would grow to be a very large animal. I was not sure how the temperaments of the wolves would unfold, and I was more interested in having a female for breeding. Cub, however, had been the pup that was more friendly toward me, less instilled with a wild shyness. He had been easier to pick up, and the first to come toward me when I put the food bowl down or squeaked my lips. I wondered what hazard had claimed him.

That July and August, although I lived by myself here, I had many visitors. Passing boats and canoes came and went; the annual supply barge arrived with our load of groceries, gas barrels, and dog-food; pilots stopped in for coffee. Underfoot during all of these visits were, as in any summer, the puppies of the year.

For a few weeks Esker melded with the rest of the pups. She quickly closed the gap in size between herself and the older litter. At the age of seven weeks she weighed ten pounds, precisely the same weight as Tyke, one of Rajah's female pups.

Esker was a voracious eater, devouring whole panfuls of dog food and giving a new vividness to the "wolfing" of food. Through the years I had her she ate the same food as the dogs. When meat scraps were abundant she was favored with more than her share of them, but her main source of energy and growth was a mix of commercial dog-food, rice, fish, and fat. She was never able to form tight, dry wolf scats from this diet, but she grew rapidly and remained healthy on it. By mid-August she weighed nearly twenty pounds.

I vaccinated her and treated her for the elimination of round-worms, just as I did with the husky pups. Again and again I urged myself to treat her like one of the dogs, and I blithely expected that this would result in her turning out to *be* a dog. But by summer's end, Esker was no longer "one of the pups." She was happy to be amongst the dogs, and played happily with her surrogate littermates, but she was terrified at the approach of strangers. She gradually became more reluctant to come to me even when I had food for her. She was afflicted with diarrhea when she was frightened; I remember holding her up for a group of friends and having my trousers sprayed with liquid feces while she squirmed in panic.

I read what I could find about wolves, captive wolves, and wolf hybrids, and struck up several short-lived correspondences on the subject. As I touched the periphery of the cult of wolf-hybrid and captive-wolf fanciers, I had more qualms about my motives and my intentions. I read accounts of injured children, failed attempts at taming, elaborate concrete-and-wire enclosures, and lawsuits. Esker's jaw lengthened, her scraggly tail was tucked in panic more and more often, and her gangly build set her clearly apart from the other pups. My early confidence began to crumble. This was a wolf, and this was never going to be a dog.

Most dismaying among my readings was one fact of wolf biology: for female wolves, sexual maturity comes at the age of two years. I am embarrassed that I did not know this, or make an effort to learn it, before the start of this venture. A female dog can breed at six months and bear young at eight. As Esker grew, changed, and shattered my illusions of a friendly wolf-dog, I was daunted to learn that she would be two years old before the breeding program could begin. Furthermore, I could find no reference to the breeding age of those next generations—would they also be two years old before they could reproduce? If so, I thought, this was going to be a long process.

In mid-September Esker and the other pups took places in the dog yard, with a pole, a chain, a house, a dish, and neighboring dogs on four sides. I was frustrated with Esker by then; I was having difficulty catching her. With me being unable to touch her every day, she was rapidly becoming more wild and shy. Once she was in the kennel amidst the dogs, my frustration faded for a while. She romped and tussled with her neighbors, rolled over and bounded up to lick their muzzles, crouched with the coiled-spring muscle in her haunches ready to unwind; she seemed giddy with pleasure.

From the small west window of our cabin I watched her play. She had become a living model of the Heisenburg Uncertainty Principle. The presence of an observer altered the observation. When she knew I was watching, her gaiety and confidence faded. She would still romp and play, if I pretended to ignore her, but her spontaneity was gone. From the corners of her eyes she kept me covered. A sudden movement or turn by me and she was instantly to the far end of her chain, low and poised.

Because of her chain I could continue to try to befriend her. I went out every day to force the issue, reeling her in hand over hand, speaking smoothly and confidently. I stroked her muzzle, rolled her over, pressed her firmly to the ground, and rubbed her belly. She enjoyed this and would close her eyes and swoon under my touch. But when I stood and took my hand from her, she would bound out of reach.

My friend Mike arrived that September to help me train the dogteam for winter. He came from Minnesota, and with him came some of the same doubts I had heard in the questions from the canoeists, the edginess so different from the enthusiasm of my friends in the Territories. I suggested to Mike that we spend some time each day trying to get Esker to accept him.

Every morning for a week we went out to the dog yard to sit together in Esker's circle. With Mike there Esker's acceptance of my own presence was gone. She spewed diarrhea, dodged and darted, and struggled violently against the taut chain with which I drew her in. Touching her then was like touching a live hand grenade, uncertain whether or not the pin had been pulled. Mike was frightened, and he sensed that what we were doing was wrong. I too was afraid for what might happen, and within a week our enthusiasm for those morning sessions faded. We gave them up.

I always genuinely liked Esker, and I was ever hopeful for what might come of keeping and breeding her, but by October of that first year it was clear to me, deep down, that keeping her was a mistake from which there would be no graceful exit.

My efforts to train Esker as a sled dog were a paradigm of my relationship with her: I tried to show her what I expected and hoped she would be, and she showed me what, in fact, she was.

Mike and I had made plans for a trip on the barrens in early December, which was to be the culmination of our fall training. We needed a place for the puppies and Esker to stay while we were away then, and over the winter racing season. M., who with his family had taken a keen interest in Esker since the day we had found the den, agreed to look after the stay-at-homes.

By late November Esker stood twenty-two inches tall at the shoulder, weighed about forty pounds, and had a thick coat of long tan fur. Her paws were enormous, and muscles like huge pistons were embedded in her shoulders and thighs. A sled dog this size would have long been in training; some of the adult dogs in our team were not as tall or as strong as she was at six months of age. I was determined to train her to harness and run her over to M.'s as a part of the puppy team.

I began with a short run from the dog yard on November 30. I harnessed a team of five well-behaved adults and put them in their places on the towline of a small freight sled. With the dogs waiting calmly and the sled snubbed off to a tree, I chose a yellow harness that would fit Esker and walked into her circle. Alertness—the harness was something new.

She panicked and dashed in circles; I backed away.

I set the harness down next to the empty place in the team, just ahead of the sled, in wheel. I returned to Esker's circle and knelt down. With her chain I drew her toward me, as I did for our morning petting sessions. I lifted her forepaws to rest them on my thighs, and stroked her muzzle. Her eyes squinted closed, and she seemed to slip into a trance. Still stroking her, I unclipped the brass snap from her collar and stood up. She remained calm, still leaning on me. In an ungainly two-step, we made our way over to the sled and the team. Saying her name and stroking her, I knelt again and snapped the neckline to the ring on her collar.

I was confident, thrilled with the potent symbolism of this act, as I drew the yellow harness over her head and shoulders. One leg at a time, I lifted her front quarters into place. The dog beside her—Smitty, a male she knew well—was straining and barking to go. I rose and backed away. Esker dove and came up short as the neckline caught and held her. She rolled, and I slipped the wooden toggle on her tugline into place.

Esker was rolling and snapping at the gangline, the neckline, her harness and tugline. I got my mittens on and jerked the knot in the snubline free. A lunge from the dogs jerked the sled forward, and Esker got her feet beneath her and shot ahead—down the trail, her tugline tight and all the lines untangled.

This was exciting, this was actually going to work, I thought as we raced along the trail. Esker did not miss a step. She pulled with a pent-up strength and moved away from her chain and circle in the dog yard for the first time in over a month. It seemed as though she was exhilarated.

Confident now, cocksure of myself and this bold experiment, I let the team fly down the trail. A mile or so on, at the turn where we would take the fork that looped back toward home, I stopped the team. I don't know what I expected—perhaps that by some miracle Esker would be changed. I anchored the sled to a tree and walked ahead. Esker panicked, spraying diarrhea on the hard-packed snow and snapping wildly at Smitty. She couldn't move out of my way fast or far enough. Nothing had changed. I realized what had been happening. Esker had been chased, pursued by me and by the clattering wooden runners of the sled. For the first time in months she had been able to flee. That was her version of running in a team—a harnessed chase. I had come full circle from that morning on the skidoo when I had roared after the wild wolf and been inspired by its speed and stamina.

Esker bolted all the way home, pulling hard, but my exhilaration was gone. I had not tapped some buried willingness to cooperate. This was just panic, with the intensity of fear harnessed to the sled. Once home and stopped, I threw a small chunk of frozen meat to each dog, and one to Esker. She dove away from the motion of my arm; her chunk fell to the snow, and Smitty nabbed it.

Mike was leaning out from the corner of the storage shed, trying to see what was happening without letting Esker know he was there. I motioned him away, suddenly perturbed. I knelt beside Esker, unsnapped her neckline, drew her up to her standing, leaning position, and we awkwardly danced our way back to her circle. I let her down, eased her from the harness, and clipped her to her chain. I could sense relief from her; how ironic that was. She was glad to be back to her circle, back to the familiar, predictable confinement of the kennel. I stood and moved away. She bolted, and the chain drew taut with a jerk on her neck that nearly bowled her over.

We had made the run, and she had survived and adapted. I could move her over to M.'s when the time came. But I was chagrined and disappointed. I might as well have harnessed a wolverine, or a bear. There was no instinct in Esker to suddenly *become* a dog. That is what I kept hoping she would do—suddenly acquiesce to the arrangement that a few of her distant ancestors had made.

Mike and I made our week-long trip to the barrens, and M.'s family watched the pups and Esker. In late December we departed again, for two months, with all the racing dogs. Again Esker and the pups stayed behind, at the weather station in Reliance. In late February I drove them back home in a team.

Esker weighed fifty-four pounds that March. If all went well, she would come into estrus in one more year. Even that first spring a few drops of blood showed at her vulva, but she did not flag her tail or flirt with the males who surrounded her in the dog yard. Within a few days the tiny drops of blood disappeared, and with them my hopes for an early breeding.

Kristen and I continued our attempts to lessen Esker's shyness around people, and to help her enjoy running in harness. I called her "S-Curve," and I would joke with her as I worked in the dog yard, keeping up a steady banter and pausing in her circle to kneel and pet her. The long, easy days of May came around, and I put S-Curve in harness for a run. With a more easygoing attitude I thought perhaps she could still be trained to work, or at least to take these chances to leave the yard.

That run went no better than any of the others. But when we got back I changed my pattern—instead of leaving her in harness until I had her back at her circle, I leaned over her from behind and began to take her harness off while she was still in position in the team. Treat her like the others, I thought, and I was smug with self-confidence as I lifted her forelegs.

Wham—a lunging turn with all her coiled strength, my hand under her collar twisted painfully in nearly a full circle, and she was away. For the first time since the previous September, she was running free. The dogs were in pandemonium, as they always are when someone is tearing around the place free. Frustrated and embarrassed, I finished unharnessing the rest of the team and turned to the catching of my "tame" wolf.

I tried everything, including offerings of fresh caribou meat, and could not get a hand on her. I studied her routes of escape and hung snares of cord and wire in the paths she chose. She immediately changed her routes, and on the few times when she ran close to a snare she avoided it as if it were the most obvious ploy she had ever encountered. I began to wonder about getting her back.

The dogs had barked and circled themselves into boredom and sleep by then, and the light was fading. I went inside to bed. What worried me most was that friends from Yellowknife were coming to visit us the next day—new friends with two small boys, making their first trip to our home. I imagined myself remarking that "one dog is loose and we can't catch it. It's actually Esker, the wolf."

Finally it was Esker's enjoyment of her companions that allowed me to catch her. She would not stay out of the kennel for long, out in the brush and trees where I could never have gotten close to her. She returned to the circles of the dogs, rolling and squealing as they worried the fur of her neck. Her other diversion during her time off the chain was to roll in the compost heap, grinding layers of smelly kitchen scraps into her long spring coat. Her blonde fur was soon nearly black with coffee grounds, sand, and garbage.

Early the next day I hid behind one of the wooden doghouses, and five feet away, Tyke and Blondie spilled Esker onto her back. She was squirming with delight at their playful disembowelling of her when I pounced. She made it all seem like a drawn-out game of tag. All I did was touch my hand to her hind leg, and she gave up. I eased my hand up to her collar, and she remained on her back, submissive. We walked to her circle. In the years she was here, Esker was loose briefly only one other time.

Summer again—the season of visitors. Almost everyone spotted her: "the one who looks different," "the one that looks like a wolf." I had planned my response to their questions:"Oh, that dog," I'd thought I'd say. "We got her in Alaska; I think there's quite a bit of wolf in her."

How dumb did I think people were? It was no longer a matter of letting them in on a secret as they petted a pile of fuzzy pups. Not with Esker ceaselessly circling her stake for hours and days while there were strangers here, cowering and messing herself and trembling in terror if anyone but Kristen or I approached her. She was not a source of pride or inspiration or mystery. She was only an object of pity and a source of embarrassment, an affront to the dignity of wild wolves.

We had come this far, and I wasn't going to give up. It would have been more pleasant if Esker had been friendly, but Esker herself wasn't my goal. I still wanted to breed her, and to breed those offspring, and to dilute that wolf breed until there was only a fraction of that wildness left. I believed in that experiment enough to face another summer of questions.

That winter we did not go racing. We stayed home, and one morning in late February I was out petting Esker. She was twenty-one months old. I tipped her over on her back and began stroking her belly. She was big, and in her full winter coat she was enormous. We had arrived at a grudging acceptance of one another, which was at its best in winter when there were rarely any strangers around the place.

I saw droplets of blood on the hair surrounding her vulva. I must have tensed with my sudden realization of what this meant, because she suddenly rolled to her feet. I drew her in again and rested her paws on my thigh. I stroked her muzzle and glanced down to confirm what I'd seen. As she stood upright, a bright red drop of blood fell to the packed snow of her circle. I patted her, stood up, and hurried to the house to tell Kristen.

With Esker in heat my doubts faded again. Finally this was all going to work out. We decided that we would breed her to Marco. We chose him because he was a proven sire, and in many ways the opposite of Esker. His white coat is short; he is thin, fine-boned, and keenly affectionate. He is a good lead dog and as fast as any dog we have. By breeding him to Esker, we thought we would temper her wildness as well as we could in one generation.

With Marco already at home in the circle next to Esker, we had only to wait. Days passed with nothing but casual flirtations and an occasional half-hearted attempt at mounting, met with rejection by Esker. She was several inches taller than Marco and outweighed him by at least ten pounds. I was ready to try another male with her when Marco finally tied the knot. The date was March 10. Within the next week, I saw them couple three more times.

That April we met a native fellow from the village of L'utsel K'e (formerly called Snowdrift) fifty-five miles southwest of our homestead on an arm of Christie Bay. S. (I'll call him here) would make a good shaman or medicine man. He makes an effort to keep alive the spiritual traditions of the Chipewyans, and he often quotes lessons that his grandfathers and great-grandfathers shared with him.

"Why do you have that wolf?" he asked one night.

"For breeding. I'm breeding her to my dogs."

"You don't have to keep a wolf to get a breeding."

"What do you mean?"

"You don't have to keep one. You just put a bitch in heat out in the bush in springtime. She'll get bred by the wolf if he finds her."

"Bred or killed. What if a female wolf finds her?"

"Maybe then she gets killed. But it's not right to keep the wolf tied up."

"Now wait a minute here," I was agitated. "You took off out of here the other morning on your skidoo and shot a wolf out on the bay, skinned it, and brought the hide to town to sell, and you tell me that keeping a wolf here, raising it and feeding it and all that, isn't 'right'? I don't understand that."

At this S. looked uncomfortable. I thought I knew why. The Dogrib people, who live west and north of here, have a reverential respect for wolves. Wolves, they say, are their ancestors in another form. They will not kill them. When wolves arrive in this part of the Territories with little fear of humans, the local hunters say that they must have come down from the vicinity of Snare Village—the nearest Dogrib community.

The Chipewyans, by contrast, are keen but not very successful hunters of wolves. One of the first questions we hear from a native visitor in winter, following the immediate comments as to the abundance or scarcity or whereabouts of the caribou, is "Have you seen any wolves?" If the Chipewyans ever held the wolf in such reverential esteem as do the Dogribs, that esteem has been eroded by the 300 or more dollars paid for a prime wolf pelt.

S. was perplexed, but adamant on his original point. "It's still wrong.

106

Wolves are wild. The wolves have to run free."

It was my turn to squirm. He had neatly sidestepped the contradiction I saw in his wolf hunts. He pressed on, taking the tack of neighborhood politics.

"People in Snowdrift know you have that wolf. They think it's not a good thing."

"But where did sled dogs come from? They came from wolves; every dog in the world came from wolves, if you go back far enough. People always bred to wolves in the old days."

"But not *keeping* them—you don't have to keep a wolf. Just tie up the dog out there, right out on that point there. The wolf will come by."

"And kill my dog—tear it into little pieces. It's happened alot to dogs, you know."

"Mebbe, but I think it would be O.K."

"Well, she's bred now; she grew up here, and she's happy here. She doesn't know any other life. So I'm going to keep her."

And for the round that was it. Throughout Esker's pregnancy my old enthusiasm displaced the two years of mounting remorse. The prospect of those new pups, half-Marco and half-Esker, dispelled my doubts. I watched Esker carefully, fed her extravagantly, and counted down the days of her nine-week gestation.

An odd thing happened. In late April, only a few weeks before she was due to give birth, Esker was bred again. Baroo, a big brown husky who was another of Esker's neighbors in the kennel, mounted and coupled with her early one morning. I heard a ruckus in the dog yard and went out to find them tied together. I had never seen anything like that; Esker was already bulging, obviously carrying pups. I was concerned, and when the two had separated, I hurried to examine Esker.

I remembered reading that when afflicted with a birth-canal infection, a bitch will sometimes become attractive to males—her scent tells them that she has come into estrus again. It was as I feared—a thick purulent discharge was visible at her vulva. I gave her a shot of penicillin, put her on oral antibiotics, and worried.

Three days ahead of her due date, she began excavating a deep cave in the half-frozen sand of her circle. It was an impressive little den. It was nothing compared to the one I'd crawled into two years earlier, but it was large enough that she could climb down into it and not be seen.

On the night of May 12, 1990, Esker had her pups. I only assume that there were more than one; I never saw them. They must have been either stillborn or dead immediately after birth. By morning there was no sign of them, no sound from the den. Esker was out and the bulge of her midriff was gone. The next day there was a plug of tiny hairs in her stool. I was stunned. After all this...

For several days the failure of the pregnancy was a heavy disappointment for me. I had been so hopeful. Another year to wait seemed like an impossibly long time. I consulted a veterinary manual and struck upon an outlandish idea. Perhaps with a hormone injection she could be brought into estrus again, and bred before the summer was out.

I consulted a veterinarian. The drug, a preparation of serum gonadotrophin, was expensive; it was used with some success to induce estrus in horses. I decided it was worth a try, and I gave the recommended dosages to Esker and to Fuji, a female husky. I wanted to have a lactating mother dog to raise those pups if the scheme worked, so I wanted to breed Fuji at the same time as Esker.

They came into estrus, but neither of them was bred. They seemed to be of no interest to the males around them, and it appeared that they did not advance past the initial stages of estrus, into the full bloom of fertility. The entire undertaking had shifted from the sublime to the ridiculous.

S. was back around the east end of the lake a few times that summer, and whenever we met he brought up the topic of Esker. I realized that this was no small concern to him. I was violating a serious taboo, to his way of thinking, and the seeming hypocrisy of his wolf hunts was beside the point. Wolves were *wild*, he said again and again.

I was too stubborn to admit it to him, but I was convinced by then he was right. I was tired of trying to explain Esker to people, tired of watching her panic in the presence of strangers, tired of seeing her chained out there in the yard, a beautiful full-grown animal with no offspring, no work to do, no hope of wildness or freedom or even of happiness as a tame pet.

"What do you think I should do with her?" I asked S., who cast me a cautiously hopeful glance.

"I think you should just let her go."

"But she doesn't *know* anything. She'll just starve, or be killed, or hang around here and raise hell."

S. shrugged. "I don't know... I think it would be O.K. Mebbe Walmsley Lake would be a good place."

I tried to imagine loading Esker into a plane and flying her up to Walmsley, fifty-five miles upriver from the homestead, to turn her free on the tundra. I would have to tranquilize her just to get her into the plane and then wait while the drug wore off, then just fly away and leave her there. This was getting complicated. My *hubris* had dissolved; I had made a mistake, and now there were no easy answers.

I procrastinated. S. and I continued our standoff, and I argued that I was bound to keep Esker. I had stolen her from the wild, and now she could not go back.

Esker's third summer here ended, the parade of visitors dwindled, Kristen returned from a five-month cooking job at a drill camp, and we settled into the mandatory isolation of freeze-up. We were going to go south and race that winter, and we were training and preparing steadily throughout October, November, and early December. All of the dogs that were not on the racing team—pups, yearlings, and retirees—were going to be flown to Yellowknife and farmed out with other mushers while we were gone. That left only Esker. No one else was willing to look after her.

In early December Kristen and I discussed the options. We would depart in one week. We could leave Esker at the homestead, tied up alone in the dog yard, with a pile of caribou carcasses to gnaw on for three months and the neighbors to check in on her from time to time. This choice supposed that I could find some caribou; there were none in the area at that time. I pictured her out there, gaunt and bewildered in the dark at forty below zero, wondering where her pack had gone. We could turn her free, and depart. There was no way to tell how she would survive or what she might do. We speculated: perhaps someone out hunting would chase her down and shoot her; perhaps she could live here on whatever we left her and whatever she foraged, somehow subsisting until we returned; perhaps, like some storybook ending, she would be adopted by a roaming pack of wolves and take up a new life. Unfortunately, I couldn't put much stock in that happy scenario.

I decided. I would end Esker's life then and there, while she was still happy, still surrounded by her friends the dogs, still in perfect health and eating well. The difficulty of the decision, and the finality and sadness of the act itself, were only slightly offset by an acceptance of what I believed to be its wisdom. I had to take responsibility for her. Ending her life as painlessly as I could was the only option that seemed truly responsible.

Someone once offered the platitude, "It's not a mistake if you learn from it." I don't buy that. There are acts and decisions that are wrong. Of course one can learn from them, be humbled by them, marvel at their consequences, but still they are mistakes.

The capture and raising of Esker, the opportunities she gave me to appreciate her intelligence and sensitivity, her physical magnificence, the sounds of her voice and her interactions with the dogs, taught me about wolves, about wild animals, and about *wildness*. I treasure the experiences that the entire saga provided me: going down into a den; raising Esker with the dogs; slipping a harness on her and moving down the trail. But we had a completely lopsided relationship. I gained richly from keeping her, while she gained little from me beyond a dependable provision of food and water.

Had a few things been different, it all might have worked out better. If we lived in true isolation—which we do not—her panic and misery in the presence of strangers would not have been a problem for her, or for us. If her brother Cub had survived along with or instead of Esker, we might have ended up with a much more tractable, friendly wolf. With a rare individual, maybe one pup out of fifty, I can imagine a wolf that would become truly tame, perhaps even work willingly in a dogteam. That far-fetched possibility would not surprise me now.

In the end, my Chipewyan friend S. was right—wild animals are wild, and should remain so.

Dogs and wolves have taken up vastly different relationships with people, and one thing Esker taught me was how much dogs have forfeited in their arrangement. Esker always had a sharp awareness of the goings-on here; in that awareness she was far superior to all but a few of our dogs. She was always the first animal in the yard to notice any change—in the weather, in the arrivals and daily habits of people, in the peripheral movements of wild animals, in the social structure of the dog "pack," and in scents carried on the wind.

Physically, she was superbly suited to this country. It was clear that with the proper upbringing she could have made her way in the world, hunting and killing for a living, travelling tirelessly over hundreds of square miles of taiga and tundra. I vividly remember running my hand through her coarse blonde coat, feeling beneath it the tight knots in her shoulder muscles, and watching in awe as her powerful jaws slammed those scissor-sets of teeth into a frozen chunk of meat and bone.

Her instincts were thwarted, but they were all there. One day when she was a year old, I watched as a litter of eight-week-old pups squealed and slithered toward her. I was wary because some sled dogs, especially as yearlings, will pounce on young pups and injure or even kill them. Esker gladly welcomed the pups, wagging her long full tail, and they whined with delight, peppering her muzzle with short impetuous licks. Those licks were a vivid cue. To my amazement Esker stepped to one side and almost daintily regurgitated the contents of her stomach onto the ground, where the pups gobbled it up. Wild wolves feed their own pups in exactly this way, upon returning to the den from a kill.

In October of the final year Esker was here, Kristen and I were flying with two friends in a Cessna, coming south along the Hoarfrost after a trip to Walmsley Lake. We were about four miles north of the homestead when one of us spotted a wolf. Boyd tipped a wing and we circled.

Below us, trotting purposefully in single file through a stand of stunted spruce and tamarack, were eighteen wolves, every one of them a tawny blonde like Esker.

For more than a week prior to that day, Esker had been leading the dogs in a nightly chorus of howling, the like of which we had never heard—hour after hour, chorus after chorus, night after night, forty-six voices ululating in the clear autumn darkness. We had been mystified by the intensity and duration of the howling sessions. There were no caribou nearby at the time, and therefore we had not thought that there would be many wolves in the area.

That big pack of eighteen wolves was moving due north, back to the barrens. After making two slow passes above them, we turned away. That night Esker and the dogs were quiet.

BOOMERANG, SETTLEMENT, WILDERNESS

I have often approached our home from the southwest, coming in from Yellow - knife by lake or by air. For a better grasp of our set- ting, though, one must ap- proach from the east or the north. That approach com- plements the other, fulfilling the realization that we live along the edge of one of the widest expanses of wilderness left in the world. Our home represents Settlement, on a continuum from Boomerang to Wilderness. Let me elaborate.

Boomerang.

On June 5, 1992, I had the chance to approach our home from farther to the east than I had ever flown my little Piper Cub. I had been away overnight to visit Kristen at a tiny prospecting camp called Boomerang, where she was working as a cook. The Boomerang camp was just west of the upper Thelon River, 138 miles east of Reliance. It was never named officially on any map; the lake nearby is curved like a three-mile-long boomerang and was named by the pilots who first cached supplies there in the late 1970s.

Boomerang was a drill camp. There were four drillers there,

working in pairs on twelve-hour shifts. Alongside the din of a diesel motor in a cramped plywood shack, they kept a diamond-bit rock drill turning twenty-four hours a day. The end-product, a two-inch cylinder of solid rock core, was lifted from a depth of nearly 1,000 feet. 250 feet of downward progress, 75 meters of core, was a good rate of production for a twelve-hour shift.

The cylindrical core samples, broken into short lengths and stacked in wooden trays, were then painstakingly logged by three geologists working eight-hour days in the core shack. They examined and recorded the composition of the rock, centimeter by centimeter, and split some of the core in half. These split samples were flown out in labeled pails for detailed analysis in a lab. A few of the pails bore bright yellow labels: "Caution—Radioactive!" The prospect being drilled and sampled at Boomerang was uranium.

Supporting the driller and geologists were four people: a camp cook, Kristen; the camp manager, who looked after all the details of the frame-tent living quarters, oil, furnaces, electrical generators, water pump, garbage disposal, radio communications, and so on; a helicopter pilot who flew the drillers to and from the drill and moved the drill itself to each of nine separate sites; and the helicopter engineer who kept the machine air-worthy.

Boomerang was truly a camp. The only buildings were insulated tents with unpainted wooden floors. A network of snow-packed trails, melting and disintegrating by early June, led from tent to tent. Water was pumped from beneath the ice of the lake, and an outhouse with a honey bucket constituted the sewage disposal system. The camp manager, a lively fellow from Saskatoon named Arnold, told me with pride that by the end of the eight-week season, after furiously hot bouts of incineration, only a bushel of solid waste would come out of the camp.

The camp was licensed, like hundreds of others each spring and summer, under a land-use permit from the federal government. It was a temporary camp, and has since ceased to exist. With the lapse of a permit comes a swift and complete cleanup: tent frames are dismantled or burned; equipment and fuel drums are flown out; and the entire site becomes a patch of bare ground. Everything is removed except the left-over lengths of core in weathered wooden racks, which can remain as a part of the mineral claims.

Before taking off for home that June day, I walked two miles over-land from the camp to my plane. It was a delightful hike. Patches of bare ground were appearing on the hillsides. I scared up two caribou, a pregnant cow and a yearling calf, from their resting place on a sunny slope. I saw Lapland longspurs, a killdeer, Harris' sparrows, and plovers. It was one of those spring mornings when I felt intense pleasure in the space around me, in the change of seasons, the firm stones of the tundra underfoot, the gentle rise and fall of the hills.

I passed several cryptically inscribed wooden stakes that had been placed by the Boomerang geologists during a survey earlier that spring. From a hilltop a few hundred feet above the lakeshore, I looked north a mile and a half. I could just make out the camp, a cluster of white tents and red fuel drums. I could no longer hear the rattle of the generator. Around me in 360 degrees was thawing springtime tundra, its emptiness and silence warmed and enlivened by the presence of the people I had just met, the pleasure of spending time with my wife, and the small community of that drill camp.

I walked over the hill, lost sight of the camp, and could see my yellow plane. Orange plastic bags weighted with rocks marked off a swaybacked length of gravelly tundra as an airstrip. This was a temporary alternative to the landing area on the lake ice, which was inundated by meltwater.

When I had landed there on the previous afternoon, there had been a drill adjacent to the makeshift airstrip. Between seven o'clock and midnight of the past evening, and with further work that morning, the entire rig had been lifted and slung in pieces beneath the helicopter to the next site four miles distant. After untying the plane, I walked over to where the drill had stood only hours before.

There was an area about eighteen feet across where the tundra was covered by a foot or so of loose gravel. A leftover piece of two-by-six planking a couple of feet long lay beside a hole in the ground about six inches in diameter. This was the drill hole, and I'd been told that this one was about 200 meters deep, deep enough to pass down through the overburden of sand and glacial gravel, through the pink and tan sandstones that cover that region, through the target zone where the uranium occurred, and into the 2 1/2 - billion-year-old gneiss bedrock.

There was no other sign of what had been done. The site was immaculate. I'd seen more of a mess at a popular lunch spot for one of the big fishing lodges on Great Slave, more of a mess every time I'd passed a place where any native trapper had done so much as refuel his skidoo. But there was just that board, the gravel, and that ominous little hole.

I walked back to the plane and started the engine. I taxied to the up-slope end of the strip and pushed on the throttle and was lifted away into thin air, as astounding a feat the 2,000th time as it was the first. I flew over the camp. Lunch was on. I circled low and a few people appeared out in front of the kitchen tent. They waved; I waggled the wings and climbed away on a course for our homestead. As I flew west, I thought about my visit to this outpost of modern industrial civilization—or, as I often think of it, The Beast.

The evening before, we had sat on the deck in front of that cook tent. The talk, with my wife and Arnold and Claudia, one of the geologists, had been mainly of birds, and of log buildings and ice-out and some finer points of home brewing.

Earlier that afternoon the helicopter pilot and mechanic had walked just west of camp and set up a target on the strip of shoreline beach, then proceeded to blast it to smithereens with a semi-automatic rifle. This performance was inspired, I was told, by the brief appearance a few days earlier of a barren-ground grizzly on that beach. I hoped he wouldn't venture back.

The talk around camp during my brief visit was not of "the f____n' tundra," as Kristen had told me a drill foreman in another camp had invariably referred to the landscape, nor was the talk of cities far away and inviting. The talk was mostly of the place, of the beauty of spring and the signs of its coming, of an appreciation for that austere environment. After dinner that evening the Japanese geologist, Juneiti Gotosun, had wandered down along the beach beyond the rifle target and milled around for over an hour out there, just savoring the thawing land.

My hardened, unswerving resistance to the whole notion of mineral development in the North, certainly to the development of uranium mines, was being confused and softened by this lively, intelligent, likable campful of people—every one of them out there for eight weeks only because PNC, the Power Nuclear Corporation of Tokyo, had an interest in a new source of uranium. They had hired people to drill the prospect and people to assess the grade of the ore. These people needed to be fed, and flown by helicopter to the work sites because overland travel would scar the softening tundra. And so the Power Nuclear Corporation would be helping Kristen and me pay for our typewriter ribbons, wool socks, fifty-pound sacks of flour, and barrels of gasoline. Gasoline for the airplane in which I was so enjoying my flight over the tundra on that warm June day. This does get ironic.

I didn't depart from Boomerang with a burning, self-righteous anger at the miserable greedy money-mongers who were out there to despoil one of the finest areas of wilderness remaining in the world. I didn't even come away with a dread of what would happen there if the prospects proved out, if a mine was developed, if uranium was shipped off and shaped into fuel rods and fed into the maw of a reactor, setting turbines spinning and powering the air conditioners in Tokyo offices.

I have steeped myself in that dogmatic anger and dread for more than twenty years. It is a part of me. But as I flew home it wasn't there; my habitual stance had been knocked off kilter.

A thousand feet above the ground, with the smooth contours and myriad colors of the tundra passing slowly beneath me, stretching to the horizon in all directions, what I felt most of all was confusion. No pat answers. That land seemed to be capable of enduring and eventually obliterating any of mankind's measly efforts to deface it. If development was guided by sanity, and by allowance for the high cost of working carefully, by acknowledgment of the fragility of the land, then could it not proceed?

Whenever I immerse my thoughts squarely in the midst of any development-versus-wilderness controversy, the hard edges and clearly defined rhetorics of both sides begin to crumble. The *us against them* battle lines look clear only from a distance, to audiences in cities a thousand miles or more from the wilderness in question, to people who have become at least partially blind to the ways in which we are all plugged in to this industrial resource-development complex, The Beast.

I droned along in the Cub, revelling in the day. I am thoroughly accustomed to the ease and luxury of my life. That ease and luxury is based on a voracious consumption of natural resources. I thought of the group of us sitting out on the improvised plywood deck, nonchalantly sipping beer in a place whose climate and brutal austerity had starved countless people and animals over the eons. I thought of Arnold out burning and reburning the camp refuse, to end up with it all in a little plastic sack. It seemed a quixotic gesture.

Settlement.

I flew home from Boomerang, 138 miles in about two hours. The major landmarks along my route were, in the order that I passed them: the esker system just north of my course, running east-west for almost twenty-five miles, rising on the east from a beautiful oasis of tall spruce called

Mackay's Valley; Whitefish Lake, with two plywood huts on its north end—one a winter trapline shack and one a summer tourist camp; the Snowdrift River, crossed just south of its head-waters in Sandy Lake, flowing fast in places with the first freshets of spring meltwater; the southern tip of Artillery Lake and the trail from Artillery to Great Slave known as Pike's Portage; the Lockhart River, rushing nearly wide open in a swift descent to Charlton Bay; the brilliant ice-covered expanse of McLeod Bay stretching west and gently curving out of sight beyond the thousand-foot cliff at Sentinel Point.

138 miles. About ten miles from Boomerang I saw a small band of caribou drifting across the polygon-patterned tundra. Another few miles and I spotted a flock of Canada geese flying beneath me, outlined crisply against the white ice of a small lake. West of the Snowdrift River, while tracing the winter overland route that runs from Pike's Portage to Lynx Lake, I circled and descended over the ramshackle remains of the small cabin once kept by the Royal Canadian Mounted Police, for overnight shelter during dogteam patrols from Reliance.

That was all. I saw no one, no sign of ongoing human activity, no fresh trails, no home with smoke rising from the chimney. The tundra, the treeline, the first ragged spruce forests, and then our place, with dogs circling below me and gazing up at the plane, the tiny threads of winter sledding trails leading up and away from the cluster of six buildings. No one home there either.

Because I was leaving behind me the little village of the Boomerang camp, a collection of people laughing and working out in the barrens, and because I knew that I was coming home to more weeks of solitude and silence, the emptiness of that wide tract of land struck me hard. Writing this, ranging with my eyes over the blue-black horizon of hills to the east, it strikes me again. *This country needs some settlers.* Odd words in the 1990s.

These are odd times. The population of the land northeast of the village of L'utsel K'e is probably at its lowest level in at least the past 5,000 years. Within the month prior to this writing, four more year-round residents of the area have departed, a loss of fifty percent, along with the dismantling and shutdown of the radio beacon and weather station at Reliance. A little over a week ago, I and our two remaining neighbors were away in Yellowknife for a few days. Kristen awoke one morning to the realization that she was almost certainly the only human being living in the great sweep of land that reaches from the east end of Great Slave Lake to the lower Thelon River, north to the Arctic Ocean and south to somewhere near Lake Athabasca.

This is an area of roughly 145,000 square miles, about the size of the state of Montana, or two-thirds the area of Saskatchewan. To the best of my knowledge every drill camp and prospector, every canoeist and tourist, every fishing-lodge guest and proprietor was out of that area for the season. All of the trappers, Mounties, and weather observers of times past are gone. The native families and bands who once lived in the area have resettled on its margins, in L'utsel K'e, Baker Lake, Arviat, Fond du Lac, and elsewhere. All of humanity with the exception of Kristen was gone from that vast area north, east, and southeast of McLeod Bay, on that October morning at the onset of freeze-up, 1993.

This absence of humanity worries me. Only through its human inhabitants, those people who live in a place and by some means derive a livelihood from it, can land gain a voice in this human-dominated world. When a land is home to no one, it has no clear spokesperson. Its integrity is then much more vulnerable to the marketplace; it is for sale to the highest bidder. After all, the promoters can tout, *no one lives there.* Thus can they bolster their case when the time comes to siphon off the waters of McLeod Bay, to strip-mine uranium from the upper Thelon, or to take up with whatever scheme may appear next. In his memoir, Alaska poet John Haines writes, "The land lives in its people." I wonder if it can live for long without them.

At times I muse as to whether this lack of inhabitants at a time of impending development is all a coincidence, or whether there is a plan at work here. Certainly there are few countries in the world as fond of and skilled at the "megaproject" as Canada. The hydroelectric development in the James Bay watershed is a good example. Nothing has proven more effective at stalling a megaproject than a group of resolute residents, better yet a beleaguered native band, about to be flooded, drained, or forcibly removed from the path of Progress.

But no—there is no plot here; that is a suspicious reading of the situation. The reason that virtually no one lives here in 1993 is simple: no one wants to. The cold in winter is breathtaking; in summer the mosquitoes and blackflies can ruin an otherwise gorgeous day. There is no indoor plumbing. There is no society here, and humans are social creatures. The telephone system is ridiculously unreliable; television and microwave ovens are possible only with makeshift home power systems. There is no fire department and no property insurance. There are no schools. It is nearly 200 miles to the nearest rough spur of the continental highway system.

Finally, there are no *jobs* here—real year-round jobs with salaries and pension plans and paid vacations. By whatever means one contrives to make a living here, it seems certain that one's earnings will forever stand in the low-income bracket. The benefits and wealth of a life lived in such a place never appear on an accountant's ledger.

This land may need Settlement, and it may someday even be available for it, but Settlers will be hard to find.

Wilderness.

As I flew home from Boomerang to our tiny settlement at the mouth of the Hoarfrost River, I crossed wilderness. I knew that people had in recent years truly inhabited that vast reach of land and lakes. But they were gone, and will remain absent, it seems certain, for many years. With no Settlement on the continuum from Boomerang to Wilderness, the Wilderness—with a capital W—looms more vital as a counterpoint to Boomerang.

The wilderness of northern Canada is not invincible. In such an immense country no single development is likely to be devastating, but collectively they will have an impact. It is true that the rules which guide development, the land use permits, and cleanup requirements, are generally recognized by even the most die-hard frontiersmen out on "the f_____n' tundra." The present policy trusts the sheer enormity of the land to absorb the inevitable residue of each activity. Eventually that most ethereal resource, wilderness itself, will be lost amidst the haphazard remnants and ongoing projects.

The pace of development is accelerating. The past three years saw the staking of mineral claims on the largest contiguous swath of land ever staked anywhere. The discovery of diamond-bearing formations of kimberlite set off this rush, a modern Klondike. New tools and techniques expedite the process. Helicopters equipped with precise navigation systems allow stakers to fly the boundaries of huge claims, tossing claim posts from the door of the machine without so much as a moment of hovering. Millions of acres of tundra—this method only works so neatly over open terrain—have been staked by a handful of people and helicopters. Airborne magnetic surveys from low-flying planes rigged with electronic equipment have targeted anomalies for closer investigation. Now the sampling, drilling, and assaying proceed at an unprecedented rate.

Bit by bit the expanses which once seemed limitless are becoming

120

pockmarked with camps, drills, haul roads, fuel caches, and airstrips. There is talk of new roads north to the Arctic Ocean, deep-water shipping ports on that coast, ice-breaking freighters, new mines for diamonds, copper, zinc, gold, and nickel. With the rest of the continent languishing in an economic doldrum, Canada's North is itself an anomaly.

Yet from a small plane above the tundra, or on a walk through the barrens surrounding a drill camp, the land's most powerful attribute is still its empty, silent space. What are a few camps, 300 miles of road, or a handful of mines in the midst of that staggering immensity?

In the present tense they pose no threat to wilderness. They are a form of Settlement—jobs, prosperity, activity—but they are also components. Each development is justification for the next, and some that can be imagined are not so innocuous. Dams, diversions, and pollution of water-sheds—fresh water being the North's most valuable and abundant resource—proceed by insidious degrees. Pieces of the overall plan appear in seemingly random progression. Suddenly a team of engineers points out that, by golly, look at this—a fourth of what we need in order to irrigate the fairways and lawns of Tucson with water from the Peace-Mackenzie drainage is *already built!* Forward ho!

Paranoia? Hand-wringing? Do I want to freeze to death in the dark? *No.* Do I want a job? *Uh, let me think about that one.*

It seems to me that only the creation of officially designated Wilderness will, in the coming decades, preserve wilderness. Imperfect and unwieldy as government land management has always proven to be, only the government—nudged into action by its citizens—can set aside and protect land as Wilderness.

Who will support the creation of such preserves? An overwhelming majority of northerners will view them as ludicrous, even heretical. The bureaucrats and politicians will muddle and compromise. Native bands and councils have a long agenda, and have already made it clear in several instances that the creation of preserves, parks, or sanctuaries is not among their priorities.

I look south. There may be a few southern environmental organizations with the strength to influence northern land policy. The distant *Us* against the distant *Them,* tiresome and hypocritical as it is, may be effective. That same voracious consumer society which demands and fuels northern development may in fact be the only source of strength for a setting aside of some untouched fragments of the North. Ironic.

Along with the irony there is an element of seniority in these issues.

The Thelon Game Sanctuary is a good example. An area of nearly 20,000 square miles lying north and east of the Boomerang site, probably riddled with enticing mineral prospects, it was in the mid-1980s considered for a change in status which would have opened it to mineral exploration. The only people who know the interior of the sanctuary at all well are a handful of canoeists, biologists, and guides. Few native people hunt or trap near its border. The area was set aside in 1927 to serve as a recovery region for dwindling herds of muskox and caribou. Now that those herds have recovered and are dramatically expanding their ranges, the sanctuary has—so one argument goes—served its purpose. On with business.

Yet the Thelon Sanctuary proved inviolable, at least in the late 1980s. It has standing based on nearly seventy years of existence; it has been out there, set aside, throughout the memory of all but the North's oldest old-timers. Inertia is its most formidable defense.

Other areas, other rivers and natural sanctuaries in the northern third of Canada deserve protection, but most of them lack that critical inertia. It is always more difficult to do something new than to sustain the status quo. Only a strong public demand for the creation of new preserves will set aside some of the places where the silence and unfettered purity of the northern wilderness can survive.

I am not optimistic. Ultimately, I remind myself, there is nothing at stake. One of these years the glaciers will sweep again across this part of the planet. Nature will have the next word. There is now a fleeting opportunity to set aside a few sizable remnants of the wilderness of northern Canada, for the children of our children's children.

At Boomerang the camp was short-lived, but the activity there was a microcosm of the Modern North. Our cluster of cabins, a few trails and caches, and the dwindling households in our sprawling neighborhood represent another form of human involvement with this place. The Thelon Sanctuary, Nahanni and Wood Buffalo national parks, and other preserves like them are a third. Surely there is space enough here for all three.

PADDLING SEASON

It is late June and the summer canoeists are setting out. From pilots and friends in Yellowknife I hear about the season's various expeditions. I know that some are going down the Back River from its headwaters, others are starting down the Baillie at Healey Lake, several parties will be on the Hanbury-Thelon. And Akitoshi, the solo kayaker from Tokyo, is going *up* the Yellowknife River, or is at least going to give it his best Samurai effort.

The annual starts of these long canoe trips always make me think. I wonder why I am so bound to this one spot, why I am trying so hard to be a permanent resident and to make this tiny piece of the north my home. Better instead to be a wanderer, I think, a seasonal traveller coming north with carefully marked and waterproofed maps, packsacks full of dried food, canoes and paddles and reservations for a dropoff by chartered airplane. Forty, sixty, eighty days of down-stream and big-lake travel, to end in Arctic Sound or Chantrey Inlet or Baker Lake... pure solitude, the uncluttered directness of life on the trail, a setting off each morning and a pitching of camp each night.

123

This morning I am addressing an envelope to the bank, depositing a check and writing two more, applying for renewal of my Domestic Fishing License, listening to the radio, feeding puppies, and recording the day's weather: overcast with fog and drizzle, six degrees Celsius.

I have been a wanderer, and I hope to someday become one again. I've never chartered a plane to set me down at the head of an arctic river, but I have set off from Yellowknife and Churchill and other settlements, by boat or canoe, behind a dogteam or on foot, to leave the checkbooks and puppy-rearing behind, my worldly needs crammed into a few worn canvas bags. I know the delicious feeling at the start of such trips, a bit of fear mixed with eager anticipation of that simplicity and that directness.

Long ago I was surprised by a statement that a Manitoba woodsman made to me. He was a fellow who lived as close to the romantic ideal of a northern bush life as anyone still does. I was telling him of one group's planned trip down some northern river that summer, and he shook his head: "I wish I had the time to make a trip like that."

I was flabbergasted. Here was a man who lived on the brink of the North, who could hop a ride to a headwater lake on a passing plane as easily as those paddlers could board a city bus for the other ten months of *their* year. He did not appear to have a steady summer job. And he wished he "had time" to paddle down a river?

Now, living here, I understand. It all boils down to different outlooks. There are residents and there are wanderers. On one hand the various outcasts and oddballs and natives who live in the northern bush, and on the other those keen, organized adventurers who come north to travel and explore. Two disparate views of the brief season of summer, two approaches to the same wild and empty outback.

There is a subtle antagonism between northern residents and northern adventurers, and it goes beyond the twinges of envy that flow both ways. The antagonism is rooted in pride, and in the intimacy that each group has established with the wilderness. There are those in each clan who have paid their dues in solitude, risk, effort, and silence.

Shortly after I came to the Hoarfrost to live, I sent word to a group of canoeists, advising them that it might be wise to postpone their trip by a week because of a late spring thaw. They clearly did not want my opinion; they knew when they could start their trip, they had seen spring breakup before.

I was right, that time. The headwater lake where they had planned to begin was choked with ice, and there was no place to land a floatplane. After much searching they were able to find another spot to set down, and they struggled through the first week of their trip to make slow progress amidst the lingering ice. Another year, dispensing similar advice, I was dead wrong. The party kept to their planned departure date, and never passed up a chance to remind me that they did not encounter a speck of ice.

I have tried to learn to keep my predictable and unappreciated "local resident" mouth shut. I want to always welcome the summer paddlers. I hope that I don't begin to eye them with tired pessimism and thinly veiled cynicism, the imitation "local" who has "no time play around in canoes."

By mid-June of every year I itch to join them. I wake in the loft and look out the window at the widening lead of open water on the lake. I want to be in a tent. I want to hoist a Duluth pack stuffed with ninety pounds of food, enough for four people for two weeks—there would be three or four such packs. I want to launch a couple of canoes, load them until the gunwales sink to within four inches of the water, drop a last postcard into a mailbox, and *go*.

Yesterday Kristen and I finished our morning chores and turned two of the dogs free to join us for a walk. A Monday! With work to do, a weekday hike in the woods is almost unheard of at the Hoarfrost Labor Camp. This was legitimate, though, for we had a mission. The day before, Sunday being the rest day in our weekly routine, we had walked north along the east side of the river. Three miles upstream we had seen that an old canoe we have cached there was nearly swept away by the flooded river. The canoe was across on the opposite bank, and there was no way to reach it—brief thoughts of swimming to it were quickly squelched by dipping one finger into the ice-cold water.

So on Monday we still had the canoe to retrieve, an hour's walk over the hills north of the homestead. We braced ourselves for the expected onslaught of insects, and set off.

For some reason I do not understand, the bugs were not bothersome that afternoon. I squashed a few mosquitoes but never saw a blackfly, not to mention the choking clouds of them that I had expected. We wandered up the ridges of sloping gneiss, crunching dry lichen underfoot, into a cool northerly breeze under a cloudless sky, the dogs ranging out ahead and back to us in sheer wonder at their good fortune. We reached the canoe, found the two paddles stowed beneath the thwarts, drained the water from it, and decided to take a short ride.

After coercing both dogs aboard, we pushed off on the widening of the Hoarfrost that we call Lacy Pond. A pair of muskrats who had obviously never encountered a human being or a sixty-pound husky swam up to investigate us. Nine common scoters, four of them males with bright yellow lumps on their bills, drifted ahead of us. I knelt in the bow and relished the strong pull of the paddle in the current. That paddle had three summers ago been along with Kristen on a seventy-day voyage down the Back River. The roar of waterfalls sounded from above and below us, and my thoughts went northeast to the six people we knew who were that day starting a summerlong trip down the Baillie and the Back.

After a few minutes I felt uneasy. Guilt—unbelievable, but there it was. Back at home the rafters for the new storage shed were waiting. It was a perfect day to raise them. There was the expansion of the garden, the shelving and insulation for the pantry. At home there was The List: "TO DO—SUMMER." The List never gets any shorter, only messier, with items marked off, more projects pencilled in, until we tear it down and start a new one, carrying over the unfinished work: "TO DO—AUTUMN." *Ad infinitum.*

"Well, I suppose we should head back." Kristen agreed so quickly that she must have been feeling the same truant guilt. I jokingly suggested that we run the river home—to save time, of course. Those two miles of the Hoarfrost are a stairway of cascades, rapids, and twenty-foot waterfalls. "Good idea," she sarcastically replied. We paddled to the bank, hauled the canoe far up from shore, and started home. Fifteen minutes on a Northwest Territories river scarcely touched by a handful of humans in the last 5,000 years, and it was time to hurry home. Get busy. Burning daylight.

I kept thinking about that group setting off from Healey Lake. What the hell had I done to myself? I came north much as those friends of mine did, liked it, yearned to build my life around it, stayed, settled, and now here I was, rushing home to my rafters and shelves while they carried food packs from the plane and piled paddles, tents, and canoes on the tundra.

Walking, watching the dogs move, feeling the rock under my boots, I relaxed. We get our day, I thought, our months and years. I get a bit more
126

of what I came for all the time, in tiny increments, and every September there is that smug feeling as I watch the summer's canoeists return to their trucks in the air service parking lot, and go south. By then some of the building projects are finished, we've banked some money from jobs somewhere, the mosquitoes are gone, and the caribou are swinging back toward treeline. The days are cool and the leaves are turning; to the north the barrens are briefly red and gold, then tan and gray, then for seven months white.

NOVEMBER ICE

When a lake freezes on a calm night during a cold snap, the ice that forms is black and clear. The lake water is so much warmer than the chilled air that the ice surface sprouts intricate frost crystals, delicate petals an inch or more tall. In the north no first blossoms of spring or shoots of green grass are as eagerly awaited as those frost flowers of freezeup.

For six to eight weeks, from early October until the end of November, the lake at our doorstep is closed off to us. It tosses and roils in the storms of autumn, as the days cramp shorter and the temperature steadily descends. A journey by boat at that season is fraught with uncertainty—ice can quickly build up on the gunwales, and the prospect of a breakdown of the outboard engine looms larger when the air is well below freezing and the wind cuts like a knife.

Now that we have made trails leading north and east away from McLeod Bay, we do not depend upon the freezing of the big lake for the start of our winter travels. The inland lakes and streams freeze early, usually by late October, and

129

enough snow falls to barely cover the ground. We bump and lurch through the swamps and hills, pulled by dogteams that increase daily in strength and stamina. A month or more into this, by mid-November, the standard line becomes, "take two aspirin and go hook up a team." It is that rough. The smooth surface of a broad frozen bay becomes a more and more enticing prospect.

For everyone in the bush it is the same. In a land so covered with water, the freezing of the lakes means a return to freedom and movement. Airplanes on skis and wheels can land, skidoos and sleds can skim across the miles to town or out to a remote camp. That first ice of freeze-up, those level acres of frost flowers, bring on a restless exuberance.

Two inches of clear black ice will bear a 200-pound man on foot. Four inches will support the landing of a Piper Cub; with eight inches a lightly loaded pickup truck can drive down a lake; at sixteen inches a Twin Otter on skis can touch down and taxi to a halt. Each November we chop and measure, until finally there is so much ice that the thickness of it ceases to be a concern to anyone. After that it is only the places of current and flow where one must be especially watchful. In spring the process resumes in reverse. The leads of open water along shore expand, the ice forms slender candles, becomes saturated with meltwater, and disintegrates.

I have broken through thin ice many times. Anyone who has lived in the northern bush for any span of seasons can tell stories of falling through. Pilots remember airplanes sunk to the level of the wings, or of one wheel that dropped in and tilted the craft at a crazy angle while all aboard scrambled for shore. All the meticulous chopping and measuring cannot beat the odds that are set up every winter—so many journeys by so many people, across millions of miles of ice.

Animals also make mistakes on new ice. One early November day at Obelisk Lake, a small tarn high above our homestead, I watched three bull caribou break through at a thin place. Heaving and kicking, splashing and snorting, for a full ten minutes they all struggled to swim and kick their way to safety. All of them at last reached land, each one leaving behind a twenty-yard lane of broken plates and fragments. Once out they stood and slowly shook themselves, swinging their antlers from side to side, and shambled slowly into the trees away from the lake.

Our neighbor watched a caribou that did not make it out. A big bull, exhausted by its struggle and probably spent from the exertions of the breeding season just past, it lay half-submerged fifty yards from shore, slowly chilled even beneath its thick pelt of hollow, buoyant hair. By the next day it had frozen in place there as the ice thickened, and two days later a passing grizzly bear came upon it and feasted for an afternoon.

I have been cavalier about ice. It has never terrified me. I have heard it break beneath a swiftly moving sled, and I have shot forward with an urgent shout to the dogs. Once on a winding beaver stream in Minnesota, where the water was kept uncommonly warm by the heat of fermentation in the muskeg, I went for more than half a mile that way, breaking ice with the tails of the runners, leaving an open creek in my wake. I whooped and hollered to the dogs, confident that the cabin was nearby, the water was barely three feet deep beneath the ice, and the air was warm. It was a game and I was carefree about it.

Huskies have an instinctive fear of glare ice. Some pups, encountering it for the first time, will refuse to venture onto it. If running free, they will hold short of the frozen creek, bawling and whining on one side, prancing back and forth as their siblings and the older dogs cross over and leave them behind. Once harnessed in a team, they have less choice. The leaders move ahead—at least the good ones do—if the musher urges them on. The rest of the team, including any dog who is balking, is gradually pulled and cajoled across. I remember one dog of mine named Jake, who resolutely sat down on the wind-polished ice of a lake on the Iditarod Trail. Sliding along on his furry butt like a dust mop, pulled only by his neckline, he skidded effortlessly for more than two miles, calm and stubborn as could be, hauled forward by the fourteen other dogs in the team. When we reached shore he stood up, found his gait, and carried on.

On November 19, 1993, the odds caught up with me, and our endeavor at the Hoarfrost River met its first real tragedy.

For days it had been steadily cold, and on the night of the eighteenth the temperature dropped to thirty-three below zero, Celsius—about twenty-five below, Fahrenheit. For forty-eight hours prior to that we had watched in growing delight as the wide expanse of McLeod Bay emerged from the pall of steam which had hidden it for weeks. As the steam cleared we saw the luxuriously smooth white surface stretching away for miles to the south and east. It was the freeze-up, earlier than we have come to expect it, and as welcome as ever.

On the morning of the eighteenth I went out a short distance from shore, east and west of the homestead, to chop the ice and measure its thickness. It was well over three inches then, black and clear beneath its blanket of frost. With the deep cold on the night of the eighteenth to assure us, we made our plan for that Friday: we would each run a team of ten dogs east along the shoreline five miles to the Hawk Owl trail, then north uphill to join our inland route and home on that. We were training thirty-five dogs then, still trying to choose the final thirty who would come with us on the race circuit. The rest would stay behind for the winter with the pups, or be sold. As we dressed in layers of goose down, wool, and fur, topped by big loose wind parkas, we remarked on our good fortune at having such an early freeze-up. Now the teams could be bigger as the mileages increased, and the dogs would be glad for a break from the hilly trails.

We hooked up the teams, five pairs apiece on gang-lines nearly fifty feet long. I pulled out of the yard first, with Fletcher and Sandy in lead. The dogs dashed headlong in a delighted rush as they grasped the fact that we would not be turning uphill. We shot onto the ice at a tremendous lope, whisked past the dock and waterhole east toward the headland that juts out from the rivermouth. I glanced over my shoulder; Kristen had not appeared yet. She had paused to change the harness on Babiche, who had pulled a seam apart in her eagerness to get started. That pause, which put nearly a mile between us, became significant.

I had passed the mouth of the river and was steering toward two small rocky islands. My entire weight was on the skidpad between the sled runners, keeping the speed of the team back from a full-out sprint. I called "Haw!" to Fletcher, and he adjusted his course slightly to the left. At about that moment I felt something strange beneath me, a shift or weakness in the ice. I called "Haw" again, and Fletcher tugged his partner Sandy farther to the left. I hesitated, uncertain whether to insist that they steer north of the twin islands, suddenly uncertain whether we should abandon the plan and turn inland on the Gyrfalcon trail, uncertain... and where was Kristen?

The ice *had* to be thick enough, I told myself. The cold was slicing my cheeks and nose, all this ice was the same age and had frozen on the same day, and I had checked it in five different places. I would just nip the south end of the southerly island. Kristen was in sight then and her team was on our trail. I held my arm out to the side in a signal we use to indicate we are looking back, but she was too distant to pick out my silhouette.

We closed on the tip of the island, and I noticed a jumbled line of small ice chips—a transition area between two plates of ice. Later in winter these plate edges become towering pressure ridges as the ice expands and contracts with changes in temperature. At times there is a crack that fills with water along the fracture line, but it is almost always underlain by solid ice. Fletcher and Sandy shot over the line, the team and sled followed, and we were all in trouble.

I sensed instantly that the ice there was dangerously thin. I shouted "Haw! Haw!" and Fletcher swerved sharply to the left. Perhaps I could run it out. We were already fifty feet onto the new plate; I could feel it sag beneath me.

The next few seconds are a blur in my memory. The sled broke through the ice and I was in the water; I knew that the lake was very deep there. The front end of the sled and all the dogs remained atop the ice, but the team had stopped. The water filled the layers of my heavy clothing. I gasped and began to kick and sprawl, kick and sprawl, clawing at the ice as it gave way in wide plates beneath me. My breath came in short tight gulps. I was glad, for an odd moment, that I was familiar with an ice-water splash and dip each week on the front step of the sauna. *Don't panic, just swim.* I kicked and spraddled. I could not believe how thick the ice was, nearly two inches, and how weak it was in spite of that. I was making progress and had nearly reached the transition line again when Kristen's team galloped up.

She had seen me stopped ahead of her, but it took her several seconds to sort out and decipher the strange image. There was my sled, tipped at an unusual angle, and my dogs out ahead of it. Then she saw me, struggling and splashing, up to my neck in the water with my fur cap pushed down nearly over my eyes. She thought I had fallen into a crack; the dogs beyond me seemed to be on sound ice.

As her team came up I could see her staring wide-eyed at me. She was riding on the brake bar of her sled, but her dogs were eager to catch the others, and the tines of her brake were not biting the glare ice. I held up one hand and blurted, "Don't! Don't go out there! Jump!" She stepped from her sled onto the safe ice just ahead of the line. Her team raced forward past the broken ice. I climbed out of the lake.

For six years in Minnesota I taught winter camping and dogteam travel to groups of students. On ice safety and the scenario of breaking through thin ice with a team of dogs, the lecture never varied: "You can get out if you don't panic... Get yourself and the others in your party to shore and treat for hypothermia... Dogs in the water must fend for themselves until everyone is safe... We will not risk drowning to save dogs... any questions?"

As I emerged from Great Slave into the thirty-below-zero wind I was furious and disgusted with myself. Kristen was concerned for me and still confused about what had happened. The two teams were moving away from us; my dogs had pulled their sled up out of the hole and the teams were parallel, circling south in a wide arc on ice we knew was thin.

I kicked and muttered, "What a stupid, stupid god-damned thing to do."

Kristen called to the dogs: "Fletcher! Domino! C'mon! C'm'ere you guys! C'mon!" They were not far away, and they were obviously confused. This was an entirely strange situation for them—why had we both left the sleds, and why were we not coming toward them?

I shook my head. "They'll come back. They'll be all right." I added a weak yell into the rising wind: "C'mon you frigging bone-brains, get back here."

"I have to go back and change clothes. They'll follow us." Kristen paused, torn between trying get the dogs back and walking home with me.

"Let's not split up," I said, "We'll get skis or a team or something if they haven't turned back by then. They'll come when they see us going away."

My clothes were fast becoming a solid suit of ice, but the frozen shell cut the wind, and I could still feel all my fingers and toes. The water around my body was cut off from the air; I knew I could make it back to the homestead. We started trudging northwest alongside our sled tracks. Even there, where I had first felt the ice shift beneath me, we could feel the weakness as we walked side by side.

"We better spread out," I said suddenly, and called over my shoulder again: "C'mon Fletch! C'mon you guys!" The dogs were stopped then, about a quarter mile south of us. They had bunched together, and their weight was all in one small area. I remembered that Gizmo was in heat, and I thought of the two or three males in those teams who were always looking for a fight. The dogs seemed oddly quiet, despite all the ingredients for a brawl. In hindsight I see that they could at that moment sense danger.

When we were a quarter mile from the cabin I looked back. A jolt of panic gripped me—the dogs had broken through. I could see water splashing, droplets sparkling in the last low rays of sunlight. The sleds were still on top of the ice. For a second I was struck dumb by an awful dread. "The dogs—they're in the water!" I finally called. Kristen turned to look. Gripped with a certain realization of what this meant, she retched.

I was running. All thought of changing clothes was swept aside. This was a nightmare; this was awful. *Think, think.* "I'll get the skidoo! Get the canoe, two paddles, a rope, and two life jackets!"

Reeling and gasping for breath, we reached the house. Kristen went for the canoe. I tore off my frozen gloves, grabbed a dry set of mittens, and ran to the parked skidoo. I had driven out on the ice the day before. We could zoom out to the fracture line and take the canoe from there.

I pulled on the starter cord and felt the stiffness of the cold engine. I dashed indoors and plucked a teapot of water from the top of the wood-stove. I poured that onto the intake manifold, took the cord again, and yanked. The engine sputtered a few strokes, then died. I remembered: the machine was out of gas; I had run it dry the day before, hauling cabin logs down from the hillside.

Kristen came toward me, her voice tremulous with terror. "Dave, they're gone. I looked out there through binoculars. They're all gone, there's nothing moving."

"NO!" I shouted. "They'll be all right. We'll get a team. This thing's out of gas." It would be faster to grab dogs and another sled than to fool with the gas barrel, pump, jug, and pouring of fuel.

We turned to the dogyard. I was nauseous; my limbs were ice-blocks. We put McDougal, Koyuk, and Blondie into harness and headed out. At the shore we stopped to tie on the canoe—it slid easily behind us over the smooth new ice.

As we moved back out along our trail we talked. "O.K., we get out there, we get knives out, put life jackets on, hook these guys down, and break and push our way out to the dogs."

"Cut tuglines and necklines, figure out who's still got a chance. Somebody will get through."

The small team of three veteran dogs covered the distance, pulling hard. Out on the ice beyond where I had gone in, the tails of two sled runners jutted up at a crazy angle. I wanted so much to see something move out there. Nothing did.

We were there. The teeth of the snowhook sank clear through the ice, and the three dogs jerked to a halt. We poked our arms through the stiff foam life vests, threw our big knives into the bottom of the canoe, untied, and moved forward across the fracture line.

The ice was so thick out there that Kristen could walk a few steps on it before it broke. I knelt in the stern, pushing with the paddle against broken edges and plates of ice. This would take forever, I thought. We talked to each other in grunts and moans; there was nothing more than this struggle. Kristen by then was calmer than I. I felt delirious, detached, and unbelieving. This could not be happening, I thought.

Kristen tried to move farther ahead, in order to drag the canoe along faster, but she broke through the ice. She kept a hold on the canoe and swam back along the gunwale to the center thwart. I braced far to the off side, talked quietly to her, and watched as she kicked her way up, twisted, and flopped back into the boat. We were still twenty yards or more from the runners of the sled. I could see skim ice already forming over the open water of the hole.

We crept ahead. Long before we reached the sled, an effort that must have taken at least ten minutes, I knew. We had lost them all.

At last the canoe was alongside the sleds. It must have been by then nearly forty-five minutes since the teams had fallen into the water. There was no hope. Kristen's big Yukon sled with its bright red cover lay on its side, tipped downward just beneath the surface of the water. Hanging beneath the sleds a tangle of lines and dim shapes stretched away into the utter blackness of the lake. I could see Moose and Kestrel there, my wheel dogs that day, their beautiful forms suspended in postures of movement. I turned my face away with a long, anguished sob.

I took hold of the lines and found the carabiners that joined the sleds to the teams. The dogs were an enormous weight—the twenty of them would have been well over a thousand pounds all together. Lean and hardened, with scarcely an ounce of fat on their physiques, they sank like stones once drowned.

My fingers were not functioning. I willed them to turn the locks on the carabiners, but they did nothing. Kristen dug out her pliers; I turned the locks and slipped the ganglines from the curved metal clasps. I had them all in my hands then, and the canoe was tipped low on that side with their weight. I prayed, simply and out loud, and I let go.

On that day my perception of our life here changed. The awesome power of the wilderness had entered our tiny settlement and taken away that group of familiar and trusted individuals. As we walked the half-empty dog yard that night, reality sank in and we wept. I cannot look out at the frozen lake now without thinking of Fletcher, Sandy, McLeod, Babiche, and all the rest. During the long weeks of complete isolation in the autumn, our dogs become even more close to us than at other seasons. We spend hours of every day with them, a huge proportion of our time. We feed them, pet them, laugh at them, curse them, train them, break up their fights, and set right their blunders.

I know that in a dozen years or less all of those dogs would have been gone—done in by debility, the stiffness, blindness, and deafness of old age, or sold off to other mushers to close out their years elsewhere. Dogs come and go, and their lives are fraught with hazard whether they live in New York City or the Northwest Territories. They live in a wonderful explosion of frenzy and impulse, without a thought for tomorrow or a shred of regret. That *presence* is what we humans love most about them. Those dogs we lost were splendid animals. They were healthy and strong, and they died doing what they most loved to do.

I know too that this accident could have claimed one or both of us. It is not difficult to imagine a slightly different chain of events. A passing airplane might have landed here days later to find only a cold cabin, some hungry dogs and pups in the yard, and out on the lake somewhere two sled runners pointing at the sky.

There are risks here and we are far from outside help. When unexpected events arise we face them alone. That is a part of living in the outback; it comes with the turf. I can list risks to which we are immune, cut off by miles from the bizarre aberrations that infect society: the drunks that careen their cars through traffic, the armed lunatic who marches down the aisle of a crowded traincar. Human life, too, is everywhere fraught with hazard.

Four years ago I wrote in my journal:

"October 8. Darkness falls on the last day of my thirty-third year. A strong south wind kicks up the rollers; they crash and rumble out on the beach, beyond the circle of light thrown by the hissing gas lamp.

"I am spending my life well. Spending it eagerly, with abandon, throwing myself into it headlong and putting it up for high stakes again and again. If I live to see another year pass and come to my thirty-fourth year ending, perhaps here, perhaps on a dark overcast night with a wind kicking up the bay, I must remember to count myself lucky.

"Today is Thanksgiving in Canada; tomorrow, my birthday. Appropriate, that coincidence, this night. I thank the powers of this great mysterious world for the strength of my body, the energy of my mind, the love of my friends and my wife and my animals. There is moose meat and cranberry sauce, potatoes from the garden. Firewood in stacks, ready to warm us through the long winter with its stored sunshine. How many people have such riches? How many people can live out their dreams in this world? How many people are so free, so blessed, so damned lucky?"

"Darkness. Winter, snow, and cold all coming on. Tonight I am here; I am alive. For thirty-three years my heart has not missed a beat, my lungs have not missed a breath; all the foolish mistakes and chances I've taken, all the bad luck or blind mishaps that could have claimed me have let me pass. I am alive in this distant, empty corner of the earth. The notion fills me with awe and gratitude.

"But not to overflowing. I've seen some life now, and it's not perfect. I am as confused and as humble and as cocky and stubborn as ever, maybe more than ever. I see my reflection in the windowpane, and I see some age there now—in the eyes, in the little lines around the mouth and across the crest of the brow. I will not succumb completely to this sentimental streak—part of me knows that you get what you work for, and what you dare to dream. You take your chances. Dreams cost.

"Dark, and the wind. Ahead is another year. Another thirty-three years or another night, God only knows.

"Long ago I copied down some words from the back cover of a Whole Earth Catalog: 'Stay hungry, stay foolish.' Tonight I would add: 'Stay strong, stay warm.' Strong in the face of all of life's demands; warm toward those with whom I share the journey, and warm toward the world itself.

"It's pitch black out there. The water is cold. The wind is blowing."

SAUNA LOGS

June 12, 1990. Strong wind from the northwest. Cold this morning with a few flakes of snow in the air. I am alone at the homestead. This was to have been the start of Kristen's time off, but the plan has changed, and she remains up at the drill camp on George Lake, 250 miles north of here, working as a cook, crossing off the days, piling up the paychecks.

Today I will peel logs. For six days now I have been at work on the long row of logs that stretches along the lakeshore, just downhill from the dog yard. Just this side of the little raised beach where, with these logs, I will build a sauna.

There are about a hundred logs in the pile. About sixty of them are peeled. They range in diameter from about four inches at the tips of the long ones to a full fourteen inches at the butt of the largest one. They are from twelve to twenty feet long—big trees for this country so close to the tundra. I brought the logs in by dogteam, after selecting and cutting dead trees from the ragged spruce stands along our narrow sledding trails.

I peeled seventeen of them yesterday. By half past seven in the evening I was punch-drunk, singing and cursing and laughing to myself

139

in my weariness. Seventeen logs, and not small ones. A huge mound of shavings ten or twelve feet across lies under and around the two crude wooden stands that support a log as I peel it. One of these days I will load pile after pile of those shavings into the wheelbarrow, cart them uphill, and spread them atop the mountain of dog droppings generated by our three dozen huskies.

This log-peeling is simple work. There is nothing simpler. I have two big drawknives, formidable tools made from the heavy steel blade of a Zamboni (the machine that smooths the ice between periods at a hockey game). The blade is welded to a length of half-inch metal bar, which is bent at each end and fitted with tapered hardwood handles. These drawknives are heavier than most, but as with all hand tools that extra weight can be put to use. With a sharp blade, momentum does most of the cutting. Still, momentum must originate with force. Work.

Every morning I clamp the drawknives one at a time into the vise on the workbench at the back of the cabin. A few strokes with a flat file touch up the edge. One drawknife for the first shift of the day, the second one for evening.

With morning chores done and the tools sharpened, I go out to the sawbucks where the first log waits. Last night I set it there to give myself some feeling of continuity, and to avoid starting the day with cold muscles hoisting a heavy log.

The trees that became this log pile, that will become our sauna, were all dead when they were felled. I have not built with dry dead logs before. I am still new here, and where I came from we built with green wood—mostly poplar, red pine, and jackpine. I am interested in seeing how well this works, this building with dead spruce.

So far I've learned several things about this, all to the good: these logs are light, about half the weight of green logs; they are rarely rotten, thanks to this subarctic climate; and they are almost as easily peeled as green logs.

It is important to warm up slowly to work like this. I was reminded of that nearly two weeks ago, hurrying into a log at the start of a cold gusty day. I was working hard and fast, feeling eager but not yet warmed up. I felt a muscle give way, a small tear or strain along the underside of my upper right arm. I had to stop peeling and wait for three days, letting it mend. Now I am careful to warm up slowly, to let the blade slide easily across the log for the first five minutes or so.

Gradually, without thinking of it, I begin to work harder, and the sharp steel starts cutting longer, wider strips, hardly pausing at the knots.

140

A stripe of clean pale wood appears on the long flank of the log. Slice, slice, slice. Roll the piece slightly for a new surface; slice, slice, ca-clunk on a knot and off it comes. I start to sweat.

This is not like chainsaw work or carpentry, so as my thoughts begin to wander I let them go. On most days they fall into well-worn paths. Money. Love. Grudges. Friends. Dogs. Travels. Logs. Other logs and other buildings. I cover thousands of miles, scores of faces, decades of life in a single twelve-footer with its pattern of knots, its texture of bark, and finally its clean white smoothness.

I trust this work. I am glad to be doing it. It is hard, simple, and necessary. I would hire it out to no one, even if I could. If I want this building I should peel these logs, and after two winters of bathing in an old tub on the floor of the drafty cabin, I want this sauna very much.

I have heard that there is good money to be made peeling logs for some of the log-building contractors in Alberta. If you're fast and determined you can make quick cash on a pile of big straight logs. I sometimes wonder how that would be. Some spring, warmed up and hardened by a week of peeling here, I'll go find out.

Two done. I'm sweating steadily now. I can feel my heart working, pumping hard but not too hard. A sip of cold lemonade from the water bottle. The wind is not as raw now; the sun is showing between racing clouds. I've taken my shirt off, and the sweat on my chest is picking up the fragrant brown dust from the logs.

I measure the tip and butt diameters and the length of this second log, dig a stub of red crayon from my front pocket, and jot some numbers on the cut face of the tip, a code for myself: 9-3, 6-2, 12-2. The log is 9 3/4 inches across at the butt, and it tapers to 6 1/2 inches over a length of twelve-foot-two. I tip it up onto my shoulder, carry it to the skids, and let it down.

I lift the next log in line, surprised yet again at the lightness of this dry wood. In this remote place where I kill so many living things so directly, the working of these dead logs, the fact that I did not have to go out and kill them, gives me pleasure. A salve, I suppose, for the doubts I harbor about our impact here. "The days of the pioneer are over..." I've said that myself, ever so pompously. So what are we doing here, at our little home on the shore of Great Slave—cutting trails, killing moose, felling old trees, carrying soil, and blasting rocks? Trying to make a living, you know; just doing what my race does best.

I start into the next log, but it is no good. As the bark comes off I hit a long section of rotten wood. Some of it is shallow and I strip it away with extra strokes of the blade. But here in the top third of the piece the rot goes deep. I heave the log aside, into a pile of others like it; firewood. Instead of being a part of the sauna wall for many years, it will be fuel to heat the bath, just once. In a big stove within walls of sound logs, it will become heat, smoke, and a handful of ashes to be thrown into the outhouse hole next summer.

I take another log from the skids. This one is sound. I start thinking about the jig I will erect and how I will scribe and notch the logs, seeing it all in my mind, and I peel this log almost without noticing it. A small 8-1, 6-0, 8-6, it is done in less than fifteen minutes.

Three on the skids. The next one is big and feels impossibly heavy now that I am spoiled by these others. It must have died only months before I felled it. The sap is thick and wet, lying in big blisters just beneath the bark. My trousers are gummy with it and my leather work gloves stiff. Dark splotches of sticky resin mat the hair on my forearms. Lard will take that off. I learned that from my neighbors.

Neighbors. I'm peeling this ornery, sticky log, turning the word over in my head. Neighbors—a word at once silly and accurate here. Of course they *are* my neighbors, being the people in the small cluster of houses and buildings at Reliance. But they are twelve miles away across this deep cold bay of Great Slave. Back where I came from, entire towns are closer together than that. I could shout my lungs inside out, fire a barrage of gunshots, set the entire homestead ablaze, and no one would hear or see. No one would come over to investigate. Are those neighbors?

They must be. I think of them often. I have struggled too hard to be accepted by them, I think. Kristen and I are the first new household to appear on this end of the lake in something like twenty years. There are fellows at the Reliance weather station, caretakers, who may only have been "in" for a month or two—as in "how long you in for?" In a few more months they will be gone, replaced by others, until the station is shut down and boarded up for good. They watch satellite T.V., monitor the machinery, and collect their pay. They live nearby, but I do not think of them as neighbors.

We have been here nearly three years. The neighbors have lived here twenty years, or twenty-four, or all their lives. We will never close that gap. Always we will be new, and somewhat suspect, and a little peculiar. Gradually I am accepting that. From what I can see, the world is full of neighbors who are all slightly at odds over one thing or another. I don't try so hard now to be welcomed. I'm glad just to learn little tricks, like using lard to remove spruce gum from my skin.

Five done. And three of those will be cut in two, for shorter sections of the wall. So that is eight, halfway to sixteen, at half past two in the afternoon. End of the first shift.

I walk up to the cabin, happy now to turn my back on the logs and slip my shirt on again. In the house I pick up the five puppies who have been sleeping there in a basket all morning. They are from Tracy's litter of ten; I will trade them for their five littermates now, and they will have a chance to nurse for a few hours. I load them into a plastic pail, carry them out to Tracy's pen, make the switch, and bring the other five back inside.

I mix up another batch of lemonade, from bottled lemon juice, lake water, and sugar. Solitude leads to habits. Lemonade beats smoking.

A sandwich of bread, cheese, and margarine; a carrot stick, more lemonade. I flip through a collection of essays, find one I have not read, and start into it. I feel dusty and warm. My sandwich tastes like spruce.

Within five minutes my eyelids droop, more out of Pavlovian habit, I think, than fatigue. I am a crepuscular creature; I thrive at dawn and dusk. Middays, especially the bright warm middays of summer, are my least inspired hours.

I close the book and walk to the small room adjacent to the workbench. It is a brightly lit alcove lined with books, with a big woven rug on the floor and a shapeless cloth chair packed with those ubiquitous nuggets of styrofoam. I lie on my back on the floor, legs drawn up, arms crossed over my chest. I hear the wind outside the window.

Forty-five minutes later I wake. The delicious languor of rest fills my arms and legs. I hear the wind again, and on the roof the patter of a red squirrel's feet. The weariness is gone from my shoulders, wrists, and upper back. I can go back to the logs.

The second shift starts slowly, just like the first, but my frame of mind is different, and I move with more patience, more acceptance of the gnarled logs, the patches of rot, and the immense weight of the biggest pieces. I can feel the drugs at work in my body—real drugs, endorphins manufactured by my own glands, those morphine-like chemicals that the body releases to soothe itself under physical stress. Runners, swimmers, and cyclists are said to be addicted to these internal narcotics. I would add log peelers to the list.

Addiction may be too strong a word, but I know how much I crave this feeling of fatigue, the easy and accepting mood that comes with this weariness. On days when it eludes me, when I cannot or do not work myself into it, I spin in circles—downward into a glum despondency, or upward in ever-tightening spirals of tension.

But the drugs are flowing this afternoon, and I'm a happy junkie with my fix. Slice, slice, slice. I'm using the second drawknife now. This log is a pleasure, so completely dry and sound that the blade has only to shave the thin outer layer away in smooth curves. Slice, slice, slice. Roll an eighth of a turn. Slice.

A loon calls from off to the east across the inlet, where there is a patch of open water now. It is an Arctic, with a thin upward whistle instead of the giddy yodel of the Common. It is a strange, plaintive sound; one of the young dogs raises his head and looks toward the lake. "A loon, Tamarack," I say aloud to him. He cocks his head to one side and stares at me, yawns, and flops back down on the sand.

The dogs are quiet, sleeping away this June afternoon. It is not their desperate hibernation of the truly hot weather, when they burrow deeply into the cool sand in the scant shade of their little houses, but they are quiet. Later, when they see me pick up my tools and walk toward the cabin, they will get up and play with each other while they wait for me to bring their food.

The knife bites through layers of these old trees, and each quarter-inch is years. My mind runs back. I don't know when this tree died, but it is weathered enough to have been dead for at least ten years. 1981. These layers I'm taking off, then, these years smoothly peeling back from the sharp blade, are my twenties. Where the blade goes deeper at the knots it cuts down into my teens, my boyhood, and back.

Carried along by this carving away of years I retrace old canoe trips, fall in love again with girls, retrace the events that led to my marriage, converse with my dead grandfathers. It is not a grim hindsight, but a vision of past pleasures and a trance-like conjuring of people and places in all their details. I think of friends, celebrations, intimacies, and cold bottles of beer after other days of work.

I think of the moves that led me here, the passions which sustain this dream, and I begin to feel uneasy. What am I doing, thirty-three years old, scraping the dead bark from a pile of dead trees at the far end of a huge frozen lake? My life can seem pleasant and logical, or ludicrous and bizarre, as I view it in the differing slants of a day's light, working a hard and easy logs, no two the same.

A distant rumble grows gradually louder. A group of several hundred people will now pass within five or six miles of me. This happens several times a day, every day. I hear them go by and I know they are there, but I am invisible to them. They sit close-packed within a shiny cylinder of aluminum, ripping along at a mile every six seconds, watching a movie, reading, sipping wine. Someone may be looking out the window on a clear day like this, gazing absent-mindedly at the ice-covered ninety-mile curve of McLeod Bay. For a few minutes they become the nearest people in the world to the homestead, to my dogs and me. 30,000 feet up, the white contrail begins to dissolve in the deep blue of the zenith. Seoul or Tokyo, most likely, by a Great Circle route. Narita tonight. Slice, slice, slice.

I think about the sauna in its finished form, letting myself imagine it perfectly constructed, without flaws and mistakes and cover-ups. It will be a neat, tight building made from these beautiful logs. The stove room and its long bench high on the north wall, beads of sweat on bare skin, the glow of a candle through a tiny window, a low murmur of voices in the hot rarified air. The hiss of water on hot stones. The rush out into the evening, into the cold lake, and the calm that will follow, cooling on the porch bench. The sound of laughter... maudlin, I'm getting maudlin now. But I'm peeling faster, suddenly eager to move ahead.

It is late now and this final burst of strength fades quickly. I swing back from it, and beyond into impatience, a sudden and total fatigue. My back and wrists ache, and no short break will bring them around. I'm muttering; I've turned cranky and intolerant. "Just get this thing *finished*, eh Koyuk?" I say it out loud, and Koyuk lifts his head to give me one of his blankest looks.

The last narrow swatch of dark brown bark peels smoothly away from this last log. I relax. Moving in a trance I measure and mark it, set it aside on the skids. My arms are like putty; I cannot set another log in place for tomorrow. For the first time since I started this spring's round of peeling, I'm ready to have it done. Do this for money? Go somewhere and peel logs for pay? Am I nuts?

Sixteen on the skids. I carry the drawknives up to the cabin. The dogs watch me go; they know what comes next and begin to come alive.

I dice up a mound of potatoes and drop them into a skillet of hot oil. I carry the rest of Tracy's pups back out to her and feed all the dogs. As I walk back to the house I can smell my dinner cooking. I pause at the door and look south over the lake. The decaying ice is gray in the evening light, and tonight it looks almost like open water.

OUTPOST

I often think of our place here as an outpost. *Outpost* is one of those words which I have always liked. It has a rough-hewn crisp-ness to it. Its dictio-nary definition, though, is prosaic and military: "I. A detachment of troops sta-tioned at a dis-tance from a main unit of forces. 2. The station occupied by such troops."

In hours of remorse and bewilderment I can apply that mil-itary meaning to our efforts here. I can see myself a soldier, drafted by birth into a heartless and destruc-tive army. Our homestead is a small and distant detachment of an invading, well-disciplined force.

Our marching orders are clear: More is better. Technology will prevail. Faster. Larger. Easier. More. Now. Hills and waterfalls are "scenic attrac-tions" or "po-tential hydroelectric sites." The migrations of cari-bou are "eco-tourism resources." The entire world is reduced to crisp, logical dollars and stark senseless cents.

Our lives at the outpost are full of hypocrisy, cluttered with contradiction, dripping with embellished notions of a romantic past that, if it ever existed, is gone. In a land that George Back

147

claimed could starve a wolf, and can still do so, we are fantastically, extravagantly at ease. Our pantry is stocked with everything from soy sauce to canned peaches; we have communication with the world outside at the flip of a switch. Incoming airplanes bring our mail, friends arrive with fresh fruit from California, wines bottled in France, ground beef from the ranches near Calgary. Here on the rough-hewn romantic frontier, our most consistently pressing concern, our fundamental need, is not food or shelter or water, not tea or tobacco or fur, but money—just cold hard cash, please. The bottom line that rules so many lives makes its power felt even here.

We are an outpost on a distant flank of the main front, a station relying on support from outside, eager for our next resupply, contact with headquarters, news of the campaign.

But out on the flank, alone, we cannot help but glimpse the other side. It is, in the prevalent view, a hostile and alien force. Wildness. The bush. Unorganized, not yet subdued, unpredictable, completely apathetic and aloof to the campaign being waged against it, it sustains itself. It is powerful, patient, and ingenious; cold, vast, and scraped to bedrock, but covered completely by a thin layer of tough, enduring life.

At an outpost the morale of the soldiers can slip. The dogma of the high command and the easy assumptions of the party line can begin to appear ludicrous and false. News from outside may be delayed, solar storms can knock out the radio, and for months each autumn no reinforcements may arrive. Steadily, quietly, the land takes its opportunity: spruce, swan, wolverine, bear, trout, alder, lichen, sky and wind whisper subversively to the sentries who pace the perimeters. Feeling uneasy, beginning to wonder, we turn up the music, tune in the radio, type a few letter...

Years pass. Why am I stationed here? When will I be transferred? What does our presence stand for, and what do we stand against? Loyalty falters; doubts creep in. Where is that fine line I came to tread, deftly balanced at the interface of two worlds?

Clear answers elude me. The wilderness asserts its power, presses its advantage. On some quiet days, alone here or with Kristen, I feel a timeless peace, a meditative serenity, spreading into my speech and movements and outlook. I dispel it and welcome it by turns. I become thoughtful, and for days at a time confused.

I leave the cabin late on a spring night and walk to the mouth of

148

the Hoarfrost. I lie back on a smooth spur of bedrock, look up at stars through a faint green aurora, and listen to the rush of meltwater fresh from the thawing tundra. Slowly, steadily, what began as an outpost becomes a home.